Twayne's English Authors Series

Sylvia E. Bowman, *Editor*

INDIANA UNIVERSITY

Samuel "Hudibras" *Butler*

TEAS 193

SAMUEL "HUDIBRAS" BUTLER

By GEORGE R. WASSERMAN
Russell Sage College

TWAYNE PUBLISHERS
A DIVISION OF G. K. HALL & CO., BOSTON

Library of Congress Cataloging in Publication Data

Wasserman, George Russell, 1927-
  Samuel "Hudibras" Butler.

  (Twayne's English authors series ; TEAS no. 193)
  Bibliography: p. 137 - 42.
  Includes index.
  1. Butler, Samuel, 1612-1680 — Criticism and
interpretation.
  PR3338.W3   821'.4   76-24859
  ISBN 0-8057-6667-7

For Marilyn

Contents

About the Author

George Wasserman is professor of English, specializing in Restoration and Augustan literature, at Russell Sage College, Troy, New York. He received the Bachelor of Arts and Master of Arts from the University of Pittsburgh, and the Doctorate of Philosophy, in 1958, from the University of Michigan. He is the author of the Twayne's English Authors Series volume *John Dryden* and his most recent articles have appeared in *Studies in English Literature, Modern Language Quarterly,* and *English Language Notes.*

Preface

There are two reasons for including the name of Samuel Butler's most famous work, *Hudibras*, in the title of this study. First of all, it is a convenient way to distinguish between our Restoration satirist and the Victorian novelist who is the subject of an earlier volume in this series of critical studies. And second, there is ample precedent for such a designation. Long before the advent of his successor (who was, by the way, no relative), *our* Butler was identified by the name of his poem. Samuel Pepys and other contemporaries frequently referred to him as "Hudibras Butler," or simply as "Hudibras"; and the name so appears even in an official court record.

Yet, having said this much, a word of apology is still necessary for the present use of this convention; for to identify Butler with a work that is seldom read any longer (at least in its entirety) is to convey little to the contemporary reader. Indeed, it may have an adverse effect upon him. "Who now reads Butler?" asks James Sutherland in a recent volume of the *Oxford History of English Literature:* "How many twentieth-century readers setting out hopefully on that jolting and rattling journey through *Hudibras* have ever got beyond the first canto? . . . In his own day he [Butler] was enjoyed by readers who were unlikely to read much else, but if he is read at all today it is probably by those who have read so much that they have also read *Hudibras.*" It is pointless to lament the fact that we have lost the ability to respond to *Hudibras* as Restoration readers did. That response was dependent upon circumstances of time and place, and unless a writer is superior to such circumstances, he will, as Samuel Johnson observed, lose readers as quickly as he gained them. Those the gods would destroy, they first oversell, a modern wit has said.

As a matter of fact, the twentieth century reader is in a better position than the Restoration reader to understand Butler. The latter thought of Butler as "Hudibras Butler" because he knew little more than *Hudibras.* Today, we know not only that poem (and in a text that is superior to those of the Restoration), but also Butler's prose *characters*, his minor verse, and a selection from his notebook materials. For this reason, the present study tends to emphasize Butler's thought and to regard *Hudibras* (and the *characters*) as an expression of that thought. Specifically, I wish to show that Butler's satiric vision derives from his observations on the unnaturalness of man. Chapter 2 — which sets forth Butler's main assumptions about human nature and defines his complex views on reason and art — is therefore fundamental to the more analytical discussions that follow it. The third chapter sketches the satiric action of *Hudibras*, summarizes its background of political and religious controversy, and attempts to define its peculiar form. Chapter 4, "The Argument and Imagery of *Hudibras*," puts aside historical considerations and attempts to deal with Butler's poem as a "satire on man," a general type of satire that is as meaningful today as the fourth voyage of *Gulliver's Travels.* The focus is again on Butler's observations on human nature in the fifth chapter, an examination of Butler's prose *characters.*

With the exception of a few minor poems, fragments, and several works of doubtful attribution, this study surveys all of Butler's published material. Nevertheless, it can claim to be little more than an introduction to the complex mind of this satirist. Its approach is, of course, limited by the specific selections from Butler's notebooks presently available in A. R. Waller's text. A fuller understanding of the satirist must await the promised edition of the complete manuscript materials. To one of the editors of this edition, Mr. A. H. de Quehen, I owe a special debt of thanks for providing valuable information and early access to his recent essay on the editing of Butler's manuscripts. I wish also to express my appreciation here to the administration and members of the Grants and Leaves Committee of Russell Sage College for subsidizing my research in the British Museum during the summer of 1971.

GEORGE WASSERMAN

Russell Sage College

Chronology

1680   Butler's translation, "Cydippe . . . to Acontius" appears in *Ovid's Epistles translated by several hands.* Butler's death on September 25.

CHAPTER 1

Butler's Career

IN the course of his short "Life of Samuel Butler," Dr. Johnson wrote: "In this mist of obscurity passed the life of Butler, a man whose name can only perish with his language. The mode and place of his education are unknown; the events of his life are variously related; and all that can be told with certainty is, that he was poor."[1] Writing in 1799, Johnson had at his disposal three principal sources of information about Butler's life. The first was the Oxford antiquarian Anthony à Wood's *Athenae Oxonienses*, a debt that Johnson acknowledged along with his authority's confession of the "uncertainty of his own narrative," although Wood's account of the poet is based upon the notes of John Aubrey, who was personally acquainted with Butler. The second source was the anonymous life prefixed to the 1704 edition of *Hudibras* which, since its author was unknown at the time (it has since been attributed to Sir James Astrey),[2] Johnson regarded as having "disputable authority." Third, he drew upon the notes of Charles Longueville, the son of the lawyer who, after burying the poet, became his literary executor; and Johnson probably found this material in the life of Butler by John Lockman included in the *General Dictionary* (1734 - 41),[3] an enlarged English translation of Bayle's Dictionary. Unsatisfactory as Johnson found these authorities to be, he had to conclude that "more . . . than they knew cannot now be learned, and nothing remains but to compare and copy them."[4] Unfortunately, this conclusion is still to a large extent the case. The lives which prefaced the numerous nineteenth century editions of *Hudibras* added little to the materials with which Johnson worked, and the modern student of Butler is, in the main, still limited to the comparing and the repeating of conflicting and unsubstantiated statements in the various lives. But, thanks to the perseverance of several twentieth century scholars, we are able to know more, and with greater certain-

ty, about certain aspects of Butler's life, than did his early
biographers.

I   *Life and Works*

Samuel Butler was born on February 14 in 1612/3 at Strensham, a
tiny village on the Avon River south of Worcester.[5] His ancestors had
been farmers in the area for three generations, apparently fairly
prosperous ones; for, in addition to the property at Strensham leased
from the Russell family, local lords of the manor, the poet's father
(also named Samuel) maintained a house and lands in nearby Barbourne in the parish of Claines.[6] A man of learning, Samuel senior
served as churchwarden at Strensham and as clerk to his landlord. At
his death in 1626, he bequeathed not only a portion of the Barbourne
lands to the poet but also divided a small library among three of his
eight children. Samuel, Jr., then age fourteen, received, in the terms
of the father's will, "all my Lawe and Latine bookes of Logicke,
Rhetoricke, Philosophy, Poesy, phisicke, my great Dodaneus Her-
ball, and all other my lattine and greeke bookes whatsoever."[7]
Though such a bequest suggests that the boy showed some promise
as a scholar — probably at the King's School in Worcester[8] — there
is no evidence of his ever having matriculated at either Oxford or
Cambridge.

Butler's adolescence and his early manhood are even more
obscure than the period of his childhood. In 1628, his name was still
attached to the family property in Barbourne; but these lands were
surrendered at some time before 1637.[9] It is generally accepted that
during this period he attached himself as secretary or attendant to
several persons of importance. Leonard Jeffreys (or perhaps his son
Thomas), magistrate of Earl's Croome Court, a parish not far from Butler's birthplace, was probably the first of these employers.[10] Of much
greater importance for Butler's development was his reputed service
to Elizabeth Grey, Countess of Kent, at whose house in Bedfordshire
he would have come into contact with her legal advisor, the antiquarian and legal historian John Selden (1584 - 1654). Butler's contempt for antiquarians — for those who "*say to Dust and Worms you
are my Father*" — is frequently expressed in his *characters* and
notebook; but Selden was by no means one of those "wholly retired
from the present." Selden was a collector of popular ballads as well
as a benefactor of the newly formed Bodleian Library; he was recep-
tive to John Amos Comenius's educational innovations and to Fran-
cis Bacon's reformation of learning; and his circle of acquaintances

included persons of such divergent views as Thomas Hobbes and
Launcelot Andrewes, Ben Jonson, and Michael Drayton, whose
Poly-Olbion he annotated. John Milton spoke of Selden as "the chief
of learned men reputed in this land." To such a man, Butler would
not have been indifferent; and, if Selden was not the source of many
of the poet's attitudes — his anticlericalism, his abhorence of sec-
taries, and his general advocacy of constitutional monarchy — it is
safe to assume that he was a strong reenforcement of them.[11]

We can only guess that Butler was in his twenties during his
employment by the Duchess of Kent; John Aubrey merely says that
he came there "when a young man" and that he served her "severall
yeares."[12] What Butler was doing during the next twenty years or so
is also largely a matter of speculation. He was twenty-nine when
Charles raised his standard at Nottingham; thirty-six when the king
was executed. Between these two events (August 22, 1642, and
January 30, 1649), there transpired what Butler and his contemporaries considered the first two civil wars of the Great Rebellion,
which were interspersed in 1647 by those quarrels between Parliament and the army that are humorously reflected in *Hudibras*. It is
possible, as Hardin Craig has indicated from internal evidence in the
poem,[13] that Butler had written portions of the first part of *Hudibras*
before 1649.

In this connection, it might be noted that tradition has filled this
gap in Butler's career with a period of service to a Presbyterian
member of Parliament, Sir Samuel Luke of Bedfordshire — the man
popularly identified as Butler's model for Sir Hudibras. A missing
rhyme in Hudibras' speech in the first canto of the poem —

> 'Tis sung, There is a valiant *Mamaluke*
> In forrain Land, yclep'd _____
> To whom we have been oft compar'd[14] (ll. 895 - 97) —

suggests that Butler was indeed familiar with Luke's name. But the
recent discovery of two letters — one by Butler; the other by Richard
Oxenden to his brother George Oxenden, an official of the East India
Company — provides a new clue to the poet's occupation at this
time which discredits this supposition about the circumstances sur-
rounding the composition of *Hudibras*. Richard Oxenden's letter indicates that at some time during the period in question, Butler lived
in London where Sir George Oxenden "did use to meete [him] in
Grasenn [Gray's Inn] walkes."[15] The poet's own letter corroborates

this statement by identifying the original of Sir Hudibras as a west country knight with whom he "became Acquainted Lodging in ye same house wth him in Holbourne," a district adjacent to the Inns of Court. Besides providing a more dependable source for the original of Sir Hudibras, these statements supply the fact that the first part of *Hudibras* "was written not long before ye time, when I had first ye hon^r to be Acquainted wth you [Oxenden]."[16] If Ricardo Quintana is correct in placing Oxenden's meeting with Butler in 1659, there is good reason to believe that the poet was still at work on Part I of the satire at that time.[17]

How long before this date Butler had been living in London is not known. Aubrey noted that, "after the king was beaten out of the field" (perhaps in the summer of 1645), the satirist John Cleveland "and Sam. Butler, &c. of Grayes Inne, had a clubb every night."[18] Was Butler a registered member of Gray's Inn, one of the four London law schools and residences of students and their practicing instructors? Aubrey's additional remark that Butler "studied the Common Lawes of England, but did not practice," and T. R. Nash's claim that he had seen Butler's manuscript abridgment of a famous legal work, Coke's *Commentary on Littleton*, suggest that he may have been.[19] Butler's early associations with Leonard Jeffreys (a justice of the peace) and with John Selden indicate his moving in that direction. The Butler-Oxenden correspondence (which refers to two other members of Gray's Inn as acquaintances of the poet) also supplies other evidence of such a connection. A legal education would have been the expected preparation for one who would enter service as a secretary or steward or who would engage in the sort of political controversy that has been attributed to Butler (much of it addressed to lawyers and adopting their linguistic mannerisms). And his best-known works clearly reveal that he knew no class of men more intimately than the members of the bar. Among the prose *characters*, we count no less than seven portraits of legal types (all of them unflattering); and *Hudibras* is filled with legal language — not merely in the speeches of its hero, who is himself a justice of the peace, but in the satiric statements and analogies of its narrator.

Butler's satire of the law is acute and informed. For example, he observes in one of the *characters* that "it matters not, whether he [the student at the Inn of Court] keeps his Study, so he has but kept Commons"; in another, he remarks that "*Inns-of-Court* Men intimate their Proficiency in the Law by the Tatters of their Gowns." A metaphorical passage in the *character* of "A Lawyer" expresses well his general feelings on the subject: "The Law is like that double-formed ill-begotten Monster, that was kept in an intricate Labyrinth, and fed with Men's Flesh; for it devours all that come within the Mazes of it, and have not a Clue to find the Way out again."[20] Clearly, Butler was more than casually acquainted with the men and matter of English law. Nevertheless, his name is nowhere to be found in *The Register of Admissions to Grays Inn* — nor, for that matter, is that of his drinking companion whom Aubrey also sequestered there, John Cleveland.

Still, Aubrey's linking of the poet's name with that of another literary figure (and a Royalist satirist at that) is interesting when we recall that portions of Part I of *Hudibras* may have been taking shape before the 1650's. *Hudibras*, of course, is a rustic poem (in contrast to the decidedly urban character of Butler's later work), and it therefore offers little opportunity to determine the author's familiarity with the city. Occasionally, however, we find a passage that describes the town's part in events preceding the outbreak of actual hostilities which suggests an intimate, firsthand experience — as, for example, Hudibras' speech to the bear-baiters in Part I. The knight is attempting to discredit bear-baiting as a surrendering of "the Cause," an action dividing the Puritan party that he contrasts with the earlier victories of the united Puritans. "Are these the fruits o'th' *Protestation*," he asks rhetorically,

> Which all the *Saints*, and some since *Martyrs*,
> Wore in their hats, like Wedding-garters,
> When 'twas resolv'd by either House
> *Six Members* quarrel to espouse?
> Did they for this draw down the Rabble,
> With Zeal and Noises formidable;
> And make all *Cries* about the Town
> Joyn throats to cry the *Bishops* down?
> Who having round begirt the Palace,
> (As once a month they do the *Gallows*)
> As Members gave the sign about,
> Set up their throats with hideous shout. (ii, 521 - 34)

Hudibras describes these shouts as "a strange harmonious inclination/Of all degrees to *Reformation*" (ll. 553 - 54), not only because together they constitute a sort of *concordia discors* (and thus ironically attach to a particular political extreme the ideal balance of powers which Royalist apologists sought in the state as a whole), but also because each voice in the chorus abandons its accustomed cry for an improper and unnatural one:

> . . . Tinkers bawl'd aloud, to settle
> *Church-Discipline*, for patching *Kettle*.
> No *Sow-gelder* did blow his horn
> To geld a Cat, but cry'd *Reform*.
> The *Oyster-women* lock'd their fish up,
> And trudg'd away, to cry *No Bishop*. (ll. 535 - 40)

And so on with the cries of *"Mousetrap-men,"* "Botchers," and others. Although discussion of the satiric artfulness of the passage is not appropriate here, we quote it to suggest Butler's familiarity with the routine sights and sounds of London and to indicate his vivid recreation of the town's reaction to two incidents which occurred in 1641 and 1642: the demonstrations provoked by the triumph of Lord Kimbolton and five members of Commons, and the publication of the Grand Remonstrance. That such writing can only proceed from firsthand experience we cannot, of course, assert; but it is worth noticing that many of the qualities of this passage may also be found in another almost certainly written from experience: that describing the "burning of the Rumps" (February 11, 1660), in Part III (ii, 1505 - 24) of *Hudibras*.

Clearly, *Hudibras* was not Butler's first literary effort. His statement in the letter to Oxenden that he knows not how he "fell into ye way of Scribling wch I was never Guilty of before nor since"[21] may be taken either as self-effacing modesty or as a reference to the peculiar metrical style of the satire. Moreover, at least six anonymous prose works from this period have been attributed to him. Perhaps the earliest of these is *The Case of King Charles I Truly Stated*, a point-by-point refutation of a pamphlet justifying regicide entitled *King Charles's Case: or an Appeal to all Rational Men concerning his Tryal*, by one John Cook, Master of Gray's Inn. Butler's *Case* was not printed until 1691 when, according to the publisher's preface, *a new Race of the old Republican Stamp . . . reviv'd the* [forty year old] *Quarrel"* over the prerogatives of the King.[22] Only two of these attributed prose pieces — *Mola Asinaria* and *Lord Roos His Answer to the Marquesse of Dorchester's Letter* — were in fact published in Butler's lifetime; and each of them was supposedly written by a different historical personage. The first, *Mola Asinaria*, published in 1659, is said on the title page to be "by William Prynne," a Puritan pamphleteer and barrister of Lincoln's Inn who appears frequently in Butler's satire as a type of compulsive speaker-writer. In this work (the title of which refers to the biblical "Millstone too heavy for a man to drive"), Prynne is ridiculed less for his political opinions than for his solo verbal efforts to bring to an end the remnants (or "Rump") of the old Long Parliament, dismissed by Cromwell in 1653, but recalled by the army in 1659.[23] The second work, Lord Roos' (John Manners') ghost-written *Answer* to his father-in-law, Henry Pierpoint — which also appeared early in 1659 - 60 — constitutes an early episode in what was to become a sensational marital scandal, culminating ten years later in divorce proceedings that attracted the attention of the Duke of Buckingham, John Milton (the century's leading authority on divorce), and the divorce-minded Charles II himself.[24] The remaining works in this group attributed to Butler include the angry "Observations upon the Long Parliament of Charles the First," "Two Speeches Made in the Rump-Parliament, When it was restor'd by the Officers of the Army in the Year 1659," and "A Speech Made at the Rota," a club of political theorists organized in 1659 by James Harrington.

Except for occasional glimpses of the parodic talent which was to follow — the "Speech Made at the Rota," for instance, is a pedantic reduction of the word "Rump" to its literal, or "*fundamental*," sense — or as early examples of Butler's use of satiric impersonation, these works have little other value than their suggestion that Butler had found steady employment as a loyalist pamphleteer during the years of the Commonwealth.[25] But two anonymous ballads — probably written during this period, and included in Robert Thyer's posthumous edition of Butler's *Genuine Remains* (1759) — are of somewhat greater literary interest. One, a bit of first-family humor "Upon the Parliament which Deliberated about Making Oliver King," may be dated at about the time of the event it celebrates, January 1657. The other, a rather cryptic riddle entitled (probably by Robert Thyer) simply "A Ballad," begins "A stranger thing/Than this I sing/Came never to this city," and ends with the wish that

> God save the King and Parliament,
> And eke the Prince's Highness;
> And quickly send
> The wars an end.[26]

Antidating the execution of Charles I, "A Ballad" may be Butler's earliest verifiable poem; and, if the "city" referred to in the first stanza is London, it sounds as though the poem were written there some time before the end of January 1649.

The publication of *Hudibras* had to wait, of course, upon the Restoration of Charles II; but it appears that, when the king entered London on May 29, 1660, the work was not yet ready for the press. In fact, *Hudibras*, Part I, was not entered in the *Stationer's Register* until November 11, 1662. According to tradition, Butler was putting the finishing touches to Part I at Ludlow Castle, the locale of Milton's *Comus*. Here, from January 1661 to January 1662, Butler served as steward to Richard Vaughn, Earl of Carbery — now the husband of Lady Alice Egerton, Milton's heroine in the masque, and the newly appointed lord president of Wales.[27] In December of 1662, the book (bearing the publication date 1663) was in the stalls; and "Hudibras," if not "Butler" (the work appeared anonymously), quickly became a household word. As Richard Oxenden's letter to his brother indicates, however, Butler's authorship was common knowledge within a few months. The poet himself, in his letter to Oxenden, attested to the general esteem accorded *Hudibras* — "especially by ye King & ye best of his Subjects" — as did Samuel Pepys, who personally disliked the poem and who sold his copy (at a loss) on December 26, only to buy another two months later, conceding that it was "certainly some ill humour to be so against that which all the world cries up to be the example of wit."[28] By the end of 1663, nine editions of *Hudibras* had appeared, four of them pirated.[29]

As the title page of the first edition of *Hudibras* indicates, Butler had from the beginning conceived of, and perhaps during 1662 made some progress toward, a second part of the satire. Clearly, Hudibras' request, at the end of Part I, that he and Ralph "stop here,/And rest our weary'd bones awhile" implies a sequel; and the reference to the widow in Canto iii of Part I (ll. 309 ff.) was almost certainly made with a view to the central episode of Hudibras' courtship in Part II. But it seems unlikely that Butler had finished more than a rough sketch of the second part, or that, as John Wilders has suggested,[30] his publisher was waiting to gauge the success of the first part before venturing upon the publication of a more or less finished second part. Since the success of Part I was immediate, Butler would surely have capitalized on it, if possible, preventing the appearance of a spurious second part by an unknown author in May or June 1663. (The latter is a satire on "Sir William B----ton," probably the parliamentary leader Brereton.) When Butler's own second part at last appeared — again anonymously — at the end of 1663 (but again bearing the publication date of the following year), Butler followed Cervantes' example in making satiric capital of a bogus sequel by working the details of the spurious second part of *Hudibras* into the astrologer Sidrophel's fortune of the hero —

> . . . This *Scheme* of th'Heavens set
> Discovers how in fight you met
> At *Kingston* with a *May-pole Idol*,
> And that y' were bang'd, both back and side wel
> And though you overcame the *Bear*,
> The *Dogs* beat You at *Brentford Fair* — (iii, 991 - 96)

and then by permitting his own hero to deny their authenticity:

> . . . I now perceive,
> You are no *Conj'rer*, by your leave,
> That *Paultry story* is untrue,
> And forg'd to cheat such *Gulls* as you. (ll. 999 - 1002)

The four or more editions of the spurious second part of *Hudibras*[31] and the two editions of Butler's authentic sequel confirm the report of December 10 by Pepys (who still could not "see enough where the wit lies") that *Hudibras* was "now in greatest fashion for drollery."

To what extent Butler profited from the success of *Hudibras* is difficult to determine. His later poverty was to become the favorite example for writers (e.g., Dryden, Otway, and Oldham) on the theme of royal ingratitude. Indeed, in spite of the court's evident delight in the poem, the only indication before 1677 of any monetary reward from the king is an item of November 30, 1674, in the *Calendar of Treasury Books* that records the granting to Butler of two-hundred pounds.[32] Still, Butler's share of the sales of *Hudibras* must, as Anthony à Wood suggested,[33] have been considerable; and such an inference might be supported by the absence of any further record of Butler's employment until 1670. Perhaps we should not attach too much significance to what is merely another hiatus in Butler's career. It is possible that he resumed his old anonymity as a political pamphleteer or that, as his older biographers have suggested, a fortunate marriage purchased a brief retirement from the public scene. We know that Butler married — he begins an undated letter to his sister thus: "I have read your letter, that you sent to my wife . . ." — but whether or not this was the "good jointuresse" on whom Aubrey said he lived "comfortably" cannot be determined.[34]

What evidence we have of Butler's literary activity after the

publication of the second part of *Hudibras* assumes a leisure spent
not only in reading, observing, and reflecting (probably the long established regimen of his life), but in what appears to have been his
own intellectual amusement — in the composition, for example, of
the prose *characters,* many of which, according to Thyer, the
possessor of the original manuscripts, were dated by the author in
the years 1667 to 1669.[35] In the manuscript material that we now call
Butler's "notebooks" and "miscellaneous verse," Hugh de Quehen
has found no evidence of a date earlier than October 1665 or later
than 1677; and, if we accept his suggestion that after 1668 Butler
tended to concentrate on verse,[36] we might place several of Butler's
verse satires on literary figures in this period. These satires would include the sarcastic "Panegyric upon Sir John Denham's Recovery
from his Madness," an event supposed to have taken place in 1667;
"To the Honourable Edward Howard, Esq.: Upon His Incom-
perable Poem of 'The British Princes' " (a heroic poem which
appeared in 1669); "A Palinode" upon the same subject; and an imitation of Nicolas Boileau's second satire entitled "To a Bad Poet,"
which apparently was also written with Edward Howard in mind.[37]
Butler published none of these pieces, but they no doubt circulated
in manuscript form among the wits of Charles' court. We wonder, in
view of Dryden's later account of the practical use of bad poetry in
his *Mac Flecknoe,* whether the laureate — who was related by
marriage to the Howard family — had seen these lines from Butler's
"Palinode":

> For, when the paper's charged with your rich wit,
> 'Tis for all purposes and uses fit,
> Has an abstersive virtue to make clean
> Whatever Nature made in man obscene.
>
> . . . .
>
> Cooks keep their pies from burning with your wit,
> Their pigs and geese from scorching on the spit. (ll. 85 - 96 *P. W.*)

During these years Butler evinced at least a passing interest in the
theater by contributing a prologue and epilogue to William Hab-
bington's *Queen of Aragon,* which was revived for production upon
the Duke of York's birthday in 1668. No doubt Butler was also
amused by the activities of the recently chartered Royal Society (or
Gresham College, as it was earlier called); for, as Marjorie Nicolson

has shown, two works later included in the *Genuine Remains* — the prose "Occasional Reflections on Dr. Charlton's Feeling a Dog's Pulse at Gresham-College" (ironically attributed to, and parodying the style of, Robert Boyle), and the octosyllabic version of "The Elephant in the Moon" — contain references to experiments conducted by the society in 1665 and 1666, and were probably composed at this time.[38] It appears that Butler was himself one of those "wholesale *Criticks* that in *Coffee-/Houses,* cry down all *Philosophy*" (iii, 809 - 10) of whom his astrologer-scientist Sidrophel complains in the second part of *Hudibras.*

When, in 1670, Butler resumed his old routine of secretarial work, we find him in the service of George Villiers, Second Duke of Buckingham, who was one of the five members of Charles' cabinet known as the Cabal. In the summer of that year, following the death of Henrietta Anne, the sister of Charles II and the wife of the French Duke of Orléans, Butler and Thomas Sprat, the historian of the Royal Society, accompanied Buckingham, Buckhurst (Charles Sackville), and Sir Charles Sedley on an official visit of condolence to St. Germains. Actually, this embassy also played an important though partially innocent role in Charles' political and personal machinations. The party returned to London with both the plans for a new treaty with France (the *"Traité Simulé,"* signed at the end of the year) and a new mistress (Louise de Kéroualle) for Charles — though Butler of course would have had little if any business in the delivery of either property. We can only guess what his duties were, but it is worth noticing that in his *character,* "An Embassador," he remarked that "the greatest Part of his Qualification consists in the Bravery of his Followers, and he carries his Abilities on his Servant's Backs" (p. 178). A notebook survives, however, in which he compiled an English-French dictionary, and recorded his observations of the people.[39]

Wilders further suggests that a reference to the Dutch, in another notebook, and a brief verse "Description of Holland" in the *Genuine Remains* indicate that Butler may have accompanied Buckingham, the Earl of Arlington, and the Duke of Monmouth on a diplomatic mission to the Hague in 1672.[40] In June 1673, Butler was employed as Buckingham's secretary during the latter's tenure as chancellor of Cambridge University; and the poet may have held this position until the duke retired from the post in July 1674.[41] According to Wood,, Butler also assisted in the composition of *The Rehearsal,* Buckingham's satire of heroic tragedy.[42] The play was written (with the

assistance of Thomas Sprat and Martin Clifford) in 1663, rather
early for Butler to be moving in the duke's circle; but such an
association — or even the false rumor of Butler's part in the
collaboration — might account for the otherwise puzzling passage in
an anonymous *Session of the Poets* from about 1665:

> Then *Hudibras* boldly demanded the Bays,
> But *Apollo* bad him not be so fierce;
> And advis'd him to lay aside making his Plays,
> Since he already began to write worse and worse.[43]

Although it is impossible to prove that Butler had any part in either
the original project or its revision, which was first produced late in
1671, his satiric interest in this type of drama is indicated by his own
"Repartees between Cat and Puss at a Caterwauling," which was
probably composed during these years of the greatest popularity of
heroic tragedy.

But we are almost certain that two other works published at this
time are his, even though they are attributed on the title page
merely to "The Author of *Hudibras*." The first of these — *To the
Memory of the Most Renowned Du-Vall* — published in 1671 as a
mock-encomium of a French highwayman whose execution the
previous year greatly aroused feminine sympathies, presents Butler
as a general critic of cultural pretensions. The poem ridicules the
current craze for French manners and style (Du-Vall taught "the
dull English Nation" how "to hang in a more graceful fashion"); it
exposes the falseness of certain literary postures (the Pindarick ode,
heroic tragedy, and romance) and of mystical learning (the ironic
"hero" practiced the "Hermetick Arts" of finding hidden treasure);
and it attacks the dishonesty of lawyers (whom Du-Vall permitted to
practice in "his own allow'd High-way"). The second of these
published works is another satiric prose impersonation entitled *Two
Letters, one from John Audland a Quaker, to William Prynne. The
Other, William Prynne's Answer*, which unaccountably appeared in
1672 — four years after Prynne's death.[44]

Though Butler's association with Buckingham might be regarded
as a rise in fortune, it seems not to have inspired in him any great
ambition to advance in the duke's world. Butler was, of course, by
this time, well beyond the age of impressionability; a dozen years
had passed since the initial success of *Hudibras*, and he had yet to
receive a concrete token of the king's recognition of his value. As for

the court, his prose *characters* suggest his contempt for its habitués. The "Court-Begger," for example, is described as one who, "when a Man is in a fair Way to be hanged that is *richly* worth it . . . puts in to be his Heir and succeed him" (p. 72). The "Huffing Courtier" "believes as [the court] believes, and cries up and down every Thing, as he finds it pass there" (p. 70). Buckingham himself sat for "A Duke of Bucks," one whose self-indulgence made him "put false Values upon Things, which . . . debauch his Understanding so, that he retains no right Notion nor Sense of Things" (p. 66). It is worth mentioning in this connection that, although Butler's writings suggest a consistently conservative point of view, they are far less narrowly doctrinaire than, for example, Dryden's were. It made no difference to Butler whether folly and ignorance appeared in the "little band and huge long ears" of the Roundhead or as the "epidemic affectations" of the cavalier, whether it was authorized by ancient authority or modern independence, enthusiasm or abstract reason. Uncommittedness, fostered by unflinching objectivity, is not an endearing trait.

Thus, while Butler was revising *Hudibras* for a combined edition of Parts I and II which was to appear in 1674, he may also have been at work on a "Satire on the Licentiousness of the Age of Charles II Contrasted with the Puritanical one that Preceded it," in which he observed that

> men, who one extravagance would shun,
> Into the contrary extreme have run;
> And all the difference is, that as the first,
> Provokes the other freak to prove the worst;
> So, in return, that strives to render less
> The last delusion, with its own excess. (ll. 27 - 32, *P. W.*)

The new edition of *Hudibras* was the first to include the knight's "Epistle to Sidrophel," the interregnum astrologer in Part II of *Hudibras*, who in the "Epistle" has taken on the features of Sir Paul Neile, an amateur astronomer and one of the founders of the Royal Society. Perhaps, too, a second, pentameter (or "long verse"), version of "The Elephant in the Moon" and the fragmentary "Satire on the Royal Society" were composed by this time, for the former work contains an allusion to Henry Stubbe's attack upon the Royal Society in 1670 - 71.[45]

Toward the end of 1677, the appearance of Thomas Rymer's *Tragedies of the Last Age Considered* probably prompted Butler to the defense of the classic English theater in the verse satire "Upon Critics Who Judge of Modern Plays Precisely by the Rules of the Ancients." In this year, too, he received word of Charles' long awaited, and, finally, rather disappointing favor. Perhaps the announcement of a third and final part of *Hudibras*, registered on August 22, had reminded the king of his neglect of the poet; for Butler obtained on September 10, a royal injunction giving him the sole rights to the publication of any and all parts of the poem,[46] thus protecting him against the piracies that earlier had diminished his profits from the success of both parts of the work. Part III was on sale early in November, and went though three editions — all of them dated 1678.[47] (Butler took note of his publishers' habit of postdating the various parts of *Hudibras* in his *character* of "A Stationer": he "begins and ends the year, like a *Jew*, at pleasure, which is commonly in November, after which all he prints bears date the year following" [p. 315].) In the same month, Butler was granted a gift of one hundred pounds, together with an annual pension of an equal amount.[48] Apparently, however, the pension was not paid until September of the following year, when the king issued instructions that the annuity be paid quarterly and that the arrears also be honored.[49]

In view of these gifts, it is somewhat difficult to credit fully the stories of Butler's poverty in his last years. It is possible that Butler — who might well have expected greater things from the king, and who sadly observed in one of his verse fragments that "Great wits have only been Preferd/In Princes Traines to be interd" — encouraged this image of himself. It is also possible that Charles — whose tardiness in paying Dryden, his laureate and historiographer, is well known — failed to fulfill his good intentions toward the poet and that the additional twenty pounds "of free guift and royal bounty"[50] granted Butler in 1680 may have been offered in compensation or as an earnest of good faith. Whatever the explanation, Butler's poverty seems to have been real. In his last years, he lived in Rose Alley, Covent Garden, a rather poor neighborhood, described in a parish report as "fitt for mechanicks only and persons of meane quallitie."[51] Aubrey reported that Butler was confined with gout to a room here from October 1679 until 1680.[52] Only one new work appeared in this last year of his life, a translation of "Cydippe, Her Epistle to Acontius," included in an edition of *Ovid's Epistles*

Translated by Several Hands (another of them being Dryden's) — a rather surprising production from the author of the mock-heroic epistles in *Hudibras*. But the popularity and political effectiveness of *Hudibras* was sustained. In 1678, a new edition of the combined first and second parts appeared. Tory reaction to the Whiggish excesses of the Popish Plot fostered a belief that "1641 was come again," and in 1679 and 1680 two more issues of the third edition of Part III of the satire appeared. (There would be no complete edition of all three parts of *Hudibras*, however, until 1684.) Shaftesbury's indictment of James, Duke of York, as a Catholic recusant, and his attempts to pass an exclusion bill were interpreted by many as a new threat of old Republicanism. For Butler, the situation created a new market for an old work, *The Plagiary Exposed* (subsequently reprinted as *The Case of King Charles I Truly Stated*), written perhaps thirty years earlier. *The Case* did not appear, however, until 1691; for on September 25, 1680, at the age of sixty-seven, Butler died, and two days later was buried in the churchyard of St. Paul's, Covent Garden. His grave and its commemorative plaque are no longer to be found; but a bust of him, directly above that of Edmund Spenser and flanked by those of Jonson and Milton, is the cynosure of the Poet's Corner in Westminster Abbey.

II The Genuine Remains *and Manuscripts*

The costs of Butler's funeral were borne, it is believed, by William Longueville, an eminent lawyer who befriended the poet in his later years and who acquired his papers at his death. After passing through several hands, these manuscripts at last reached Robert Thyer, keeper of the public library in Manchester, who in 1759 published portions of these materials in two volumes entitled *The Genuine Remains in Verse and Prose of Mr. Samuel Butler*. Earlier, in 1715, 1716, and 1717, three volumes entitled *The Posthumous Works in Prose and Verse of Mr. Samuel Butler* had appeared. The latter can only be regarded as a bookseller's attempt to capitalize upon Butler's enduring fame. Of the works attributed to Butler in these volumes, only five are held today to be his — the ode *To the Memory of the Most Renowned Du-Vall; The Case of King Charles I; Two Letters, One from John Audland . . . The Other, William Prynne's Answer; Mola Asinaria;* and *Mercurius Menippeus. The Loyal Satyrist, or Hudibras in Prose*, elsewhere subtitled *Memoirs of the Years 1649 and 1650*. This last work is, in my opinion, not Butler's; for the strength of its attribution merely rests upon a

number of verse echoes from *Hudibras* and upon a reference to Sir
Samuel Luke, once the supposed inspiration of that poem. The contents of *The Genuine Remains*, however, are generally accepted as
authentic Butler. Thyer's first volume includes 121 of the poet's
prose *characters* (never printed in the author's life) and selections
from his notebook. His second volume includes all but three — *Mola
Asinaria, Lord Roos His Answer* . . . , and *Mercurius Menippeus* —
of the minor works mentioned in the present chapter and a number
of less familiar pieces of verse.

Among these minor works, we might call attention to several formal verse satires: "Upon Gaming," "On Our Ridiculous Imitation of
the French," "Upon Drunkenness," "Upon Marriage," "Upon
Plagiaries." "Upon the Imperfection and Abuse of Human Learning" (with its fragmentary second part), and "Upon the Weakness
and Misery of Man." Also noteworthy are the informal piece "Upon
Philip Nye's Thanksgiving Beard" and two mock-Pindarick odes —
"Upon an Hypocritical Non-conformist" and "Upon Modern
Critics." Although only five of these poems are written in the rough
octosyllabic couplet which we have come to identify with Butler, and
although the two last-mentioned formal satires lack his typical sense
of humor, all are no doubt his. Butler has dealt with six of their subjects in his prose characters, and Philip Nye's "Thanksgiving Beard"
is mentioned specifically in the "Heroical Epistle of Hudibras to his
Lady" (l. 188). As for the two more serious satires on men and learning, we need only turn to Butler's notebook reflections in prose and
in verse to find their counterparts.

In 1885, Butler's manuscripts, or what remained of them (Thyer's
Genuine Remains is now our only source of some of Butler's verse),
were acquired by the British Museum. These consist of two folio
volumes: one is in Butler's own hand (Add. MSS. 32625); the other is
believed to be Thyer's transcriptions of extracts from original
manuscripts (Add. MSS. 32626). A third manuscript volume, which
is described by Treadway Russell Nash in his 1793 edition of
Hudibras as Butler's commonplace book, disappeared from scholarly
attention until 1941 when Dr. A. S. W. Rosenbach listed it in his
catalogue of *English Poetry to 1700*. In 1944, Norma Bentley studied
the commonplace book in her doctoral dissertation on Butler.
Although she found evidence of another hand and of later revisions
in the manuscript (contributions of its first owner, William
Longueville), and although it was impossible during World War II
to compare the older handwriting of the manuscripts with Butler's

authentic script, Miss Bentley assumed "the greater part of the Commonplace Book to be Butler's."[53] Thus the matter remained until very recently when Hugh de Quehen, who is currently editing all Butler's manuscript material, determined that the commonplace book is merely a transcription by William Longueville of passages of interest to him in the original manuscripts received at Butler's death.[54] Nevertheless, the extent of the authentic holograph manuscript is considerable — according to de Quehen, "15,700 lines of miscellaneous verse and a thousand passages of miscellaneous prose averaging about ninety words per passage," much of it not yet published. Moreover, Longueville's manuscript commonplace book preserves an additional 180 unique passages transcribed from manuscripts now lost.[55]

The so-called "notebook" material which we consider in the next chapter (only a fraction of the mass de Quehen has compiled) was arranged by Butler under thirteen general headings: "Learning and Knowledge," "Truth and Falshood," "Religion," "Wit and Folly," "Ignorance," "Reason," "Virtue and Vice," "Opinion," "Nature," "History," "Physique," "Princes and Government," and "Criticisms upon Books and Authors." (Thyer grouped additional passages under the heading "Sundry Thoughts.") It is unlikely that this collection of materials — some of it like Baconian aphorisms; some of it like short essays — was ever intended by Butler for publication. More probably, it served as a convenient means of keeping at hand witty or thoughtful elaborations of personal insights and reflection for inclusion in other works. Dr. Johnson may have suggested this possibility when he described the materials in Thyer's possession as "*Hudibras* in prose," a repository of "thoughts that were generated in his own mind [which] might be usefully applied to some future purpose."[56] For example, under the heading "Religion" in the notebook, Butler noted the following: "Because the Scripture says obedience is better then Sacrifice, sectarys believe the loss of it will serve" (295:6). If this statement is incomprehensible, it is due either to the editorial fidelity or to the laziness of the transcriber of the manuscript — A. R. Waller, whose text of the notebook we shall be quoting in this study — for he had two opportunities to correct his error. In the *character* of "An Hypocritical Nonconformist," Butler wrote "And because the Scripture says, *Obedience is better than Sacrifice,* he believes the less of it will serve" (p. 48). Again in the *character* of "An Anabaptist," we read "He believes, because Obedience is better than Sacrifice, the less of it will serve" (p. 217).

Just below the passage on sectarian obedience in the notebook, we read that "Presbyterians cry down the Common Prayer because there is no Ostentation of Gifts in it, with which the People are most taken, and therefore they esteeme it but as lost time" (295:7); and then, among the *characters*, we read that an "Hypocritical Noncon-formist" "cries down the Common-Prayer, because there is no Ostentation of Gifts to be used in the reading of it, without which he esteems it no better than mere loss of Time, and Labour in Vain, that brings him in no Return of Interest and Vain-Glory from the Rabble" (p. 49). Such passages in the *characters* (and there are dozens of other examples) probably constitute a third stage in the refinement of Butler's observations. The final folios placed in the British Museum consist of a collection of unclassified notes in rather rougher form than the classified notes that precede them. These appear to be Butler's original jottings which, Professor de Quehen argues, he gradually "transferred with minor alterations to the classified groups"[57] and then introduced into specific works.

It seems likely that Butler followed a similar procedure in the composition of verse, although the unstated editorial practices of René Lamar[58] — the Cambridge editor of Butler's minor verse — make illustration at the present time impossible. Lamar's policy of rearranging passages also conceals the presence of at least one em-bryonic poem in the manuscript material. When Josephine Bauer discovered 252 lines of a narrative satire on medicine[59] in several numbers of the *London Magazine* for 1825 - 26, she relocated all but a few of the lines under the heading "Physique" in the "Thesaurus" or appendix of Lamar's edition of the minor verse. The story, we might notice in passing, concerns a doctor, who had discovered a "Universal Cure, for all Diseases," and his wife, who was given as her household allowance only those fees her husband received for curing patients of one "slight Disease." "*She must have more Diseases of her own*," she complains to her husband, who angrily observes that the perversity of women is the one disease his panacea cannot cure. The wife reminds her doctor-husband of his dependence upon the "Little Beggerly Infirmities" of her sex; for his earliest success was built upon the treatment of venereal disease. Forced to concede the truth of this statement, the doctor must change his defense: the operating costs of quackery are high; so it is necessary to employ thrift in the management of household affairs. Here, the sequence ends; but whether Butler left the poem un-finished or continued it in verses not recognized as belonging to it cannot now be determined. Our answer to this question and to many others concerning Butler's working methods must await the forthcoming publication of all the extant manuscript materials.

CHAPTER 2

Butler's Thought

FOR Butler, as for his era, the terms "nature" and, with certain empiricist qualifications, "reason" expressed the traditional optimistic sanctions of both intelligibility in the universe and intelligence in man. Butler believed that "the original of Reason proceeds from the Divine wisdome"; that "the Order of Nature is but a Copie which the Divine wisdome has drawn of itself, and committed to the Custody of Nature"; and that man alone "has the Honor, and Priviledge" to read "this Booke of Nature . . . which lead's him immediatly to God" (337:1). Thus, in nature's order and in man's awareness of his own place within it, there lies all the knowledge needed in this world.

But theoretical regularity did not blind Butler to the real ambiguities in men. Though nature's variations are all comformable to general law, "the variations of [human] Reason" are not (336:2). The very fact that truth "has no variations to be allow'd for, nor alterations from its own originall Simplicity," seemed to him to make it not inviolable but only more susceptible to the undermining of falsehood, which "has change of faces and every one proof against all impression" (293:4). Butler assayed "the Generall Temper of mankind" as "a Mixture of Cheat and Folly"; and reason — far from leading man to truth — often merely exchanges the real world for "another Kinde of Fooles Paradise of what should be, not what is" (276:1). Indeed, Butler's observations about men appear to contradict the rational harmony of man and Nature that is implicit in the philosophical assumptions of his era. Ricardo Quintana has suggested that Butler avoided coming to grips with this contradiction: Butler "never genuinely asked," he writes, "why it should be that truth is attainable only through the cautious and rigorous exercise of reason, and that in consequence the world lies subject to all the 'variations of reason' brought in by the fools and knaves." Quintana argues that Butler's belief in a rational order throughout nature prevented him from naturalizing human defects; therefore, the human tendency to violate that order could be regarded by him only as "essentially unnatural."[1] Although Butler did fail to resolve this paradox, it must also be said that he was very much aware of it. Indeed, his conviction that man is unnatural but *not irrational* is one of the central tenets of his theory of human nature.

I *Reason*

Butler himself has suggested an approach to the paradox of man's unnaturalness in his peculiar interpretation of the myth of the Fall of Man — specifically, in his assertion that "man was not created Rationall" (456:4); that Adam's innocence (the capacity to believe without understanding) was tantamount to what, in the world of the fallen, would be termed ignorance (333:1; 284:6); and that reason, purchased in the fall, was to become not only the means of man's redemption, but also — and most importantly — the means of his punishment. Contrary to many seventeenth century thinkers who interpreted the loss of paradise as a forfeiture or impairment of superior intellectual powers, Butler apparently felt that Adam lost only the "priviledges" of ease and innocence with Eden. The Restoration philosopher Joseph Glanvill, for example, believed that "the human understanding and senses suffered a simultaneous jar at the Fall which threw them out of the perfect prelapsarian focus which made Adam the envy of the angels."[2] Animals, he believed, "are probably less inferior to us in wisdom than we are to Adam."[3] For Butler, however, the innocent Adam understood little more than the animals; for "Providence" supplied for all creatures before the Fall what they lacked in mind (326:2; 329:1). The Fall itself, he believed, was an error that demonstrated the absence of Adam's sense and judgment; "for if his eies had been open before he tasted the Forbidden Fruite, He would never have forfeited the whole Orchard of Paradise for one Apple of it" (284:5). By believing Satan's promise that he could know what God knows — by ignoring, that is, the differences between man and God — Adam had accepted for truth what Butler and his century were to call "opinion" (456:4), a form of self-flattery or intellectual indulgence (278:1) to which ignorance (and hence innocence) is especially susceptible. "He that know's nothing," Butler wrote, "knows as little of himself, and ha's no more Sense of his own defects then he has of anything else, which renders him impregnable against all Conviction, which no reason can promise it self" (333:2). Far from suffering an eclipse, then, "the eies of Adam's understanding" were for the first time opened at the Fall. This is not to say that Butler believed Paradise well lost. Perhaps he would have if Adam had not forfeited the tree ("the most compendious way of attaining" knowledge) along with the garden (288:1). But, in affording man the means of acquiring knowledge himself, the tree also laid upon him the Godlike responsibility of distinguishing between truth and falsehood — from Butler's point of view, an extremely difficult task for human sense and reason.

Thus, according to Butler, God sentenced only certain men to physical labor, but certain others (those endowed with particular intellectual abilities) to mental labor, to "Study, observation, and Practice" in "as hard and barren a Soyl" as the earth was to those condemned to physical punishment (288:1). Henceforth, man would purchase knowledge as well as bread by his own efforts; he would become "a Slave to his own condition . . . forcd to drudge for that Food and Cloathing which other creatures receive freely from the Bounty of Nature" (363:3). This passage, included under the rubric "Nature" in Butler's notebook, refers, of course, to man's physical difficulties; there are other passages, however, that refer to the spiritual and intellectual difficulties he shall encounter. A note in the manuscript commonplace book (and then incorporated in the "Satire Upon the Imperfection and Abuse of Human Learning") about the fruitless pains of linguistic study in the sciences continues as follows:

y^c variation of Languages at ye Building of Babell was but a 2^d Curse vpon ye fall of man And as ye first brought him knowledge at ye Charge of Labour & Drudgery in tilling ye Earth that was rendered Barren of purpose only to find him worke & in ye end to devoure Him. So do's this 2^d of Learning Languages afford him a very pittifull Returne of Knowledge in comparison of y^c intollerable Paines & Industry y^t is spent vpon It, for wch hee w^d have nothing but his Labour for his paines if hee did not Divert himself with setting false values vpon some little Things.[4]

In a section of the notebook entitled "Wit and Folly," Butler remarks that, after nature gave men reason, she provided them with "neither Food, nor Cloaths, nor Armes (as she has don Beasts at her own Charge) *but such as they can invent, and prepare for themselves*" (326:2 — italics added); and, under "Learning and Knowledge," he observes that men "do but more plainly perceive, their own wants and Nakedness, as he did, which before in the State of Ignorance [Butler's phrase for *the State of Innocence*], were hidden from him, untill the eies of his understanding were opened, only to let him see his losses, and the Miseries which he had betrayd himself unto" (284:6).

But the bitter realization of human imperfection was, for Butler, only a part of the intellectual punishment of fallen man. Indeed, if Adam's first rational perception was of his "own wants and Nakedness," one of his first rational acts must have been his invention of clothing to conceal these truths about his nature. Like "a spruce Gallant," Butler notes, man "take's his cloaths for the better Part of his Redemption; For as Adam after his Fall among his other Defects found himself Naked (of which he appeard to be most Sensible and hid himself) so his Restoration from that Calamity, and Improvment of it into Bravery, cannot but apeare to him to be his greatest Indulgence" (457:1). These "indulgences" — the "setting [of] false values upon some little Things," as he described them in his note on the pains of linguistic study — Butler regarded as the causes of strife in learning, theology, and law. Thus, man himself deliberately confounds truth and falsehood; and, in so doing, he becomes the agent of his own punishment.

We may learn more of Butler's view of the intellectual punishment of fallen man by paying closer attention, therefore, to those passages in his writing which refer to clothing or to its absence. Sartorial ineptness and extravagance have of course always been commonplaces of comedy: in Butler's works, we think of the inventory of Hudibras' external accouterments, of the attention to dress in the prose *characters* (two of which, the "Huffing Courtier" and the "Fantastic," are wholly delineated in these terms) and in the "Satire on Our Ridiculous Imitation of the French." But such details do more than merely caricature extremes of fashion, for Hudibras' hose conceal that common human need that conventional literary knights of the road seem able to ignore: "He alwayes chose/To carry Vittle in his hose" (I, i, 315 - 16); and the "Huffing Courtier" — who is the latest creation of his tailor — finds in clothes the regeneration of his original nature: "He is very careful to discover the Lining of his Coat, that you may not suspect any Want of Integrity or Flaw in him from the Skin outwards" (p. 70). "Clothing," writes Paul Fussell in his study of Augustan Humanism, "is the achievement of civilization, but the achievement of a high civilization is the creation of a symbolic clothing of conventions and institutions."[5] Like Jonathan Swift, Butler traced the moral and intellectual history of man in his creation of symbolic clothing: learned languages, "hard" words, cant, cabalistical and legal terms, literature, myth, religions, philosophical systems, and — especially — individual opinions — all are metaphorically treated in terms of clothing. But, whereas the humanists regarded such clothing as the "motive of noble and social action,"[6] Butler saw it as the motive of deception and hypocrisy, as the occasion for many of those difficult judgments which "so fruitfully stocked" the world of knowledge after the Fall.

Butler would have agreed with the Humanists that clothing (in both the literal and symbolic sense) was indispensible in a world from which God had withdrawn his providential care of man. The "Taylers Trad," he notes under the rubric "Contradictions," was instituted "by God himselfe next after he made woeman to make her and her husband Coats of Skins, after they had Try'd to fit themselves with suites of figleavs" (439:1): and, as we shall see, Butler himself regarded wit and fancy as "the Cloaths, and Ornaments of Judgment" (328:2),. In such cases, a clear distinction is drawn between clothes and the thing clothed: Adam's suit did not alter his essential frailty; and true wit is made to contribute to "the Benefit and advantage of [the] Truth" it adorns (336:1). But, again like Swift, Butler felt that this distinction was frequently ignored. Just as Gulliver used clothing to conceal his kinship with the Yahoo, so most men have turned this sign of their fallen condition to their own credit, "as if they gaind not lost by it, and had made themselves finer then ever God meand they should bee" (476:1). Thus, Butler wrote in the "Satire upon the Weakness and Misery of Man":

> Our bravery's but a vain disguise,
> To hide us from the world's dull eyes,
> The remedy of a defect,
> With which our nakedness is deckt;
> Yet makes us swell with pride, and boast,
> As if we'd gain'd by being lost. (ll. 89 - 94, *P. W.*)

And, as the means of satisfying the human desire to think well of oneself also serve the desire to be thought well of by others, men soon learned to cover the "Lineing" of vice worn "next their Bodys, for ease and convenience" with an outer dress of virtue "for show" (341:4). Butler frequently draws upon this contrast between the outer and inner man (symbolically, the clothed and unclothed man); and the most obvious instance occurs in Part II of *Hudibras* where the knight, who falsely claims to have endured a whipping for his mistress, fears that she will "make me pull my *Dublet* off" (iii, 82) and uncover the truth. Clothed, Hudibras appears as the champion of "*Faith*, and *Love*, and *Honour*"; stripped, he "shall be reduc'd t'a Knight oth' Post [a professional perjurer]" (iii, 87 - 88). "All Bewty, and the Ornaments of it," Butler observed in perhaps the most Swiftian passage in the notebook, "are Naturally designed for the outsides of things, and not their inward Parts: For if the Inside of the Bewtifullest Creature in the World were turnd outward, nothing could appear more Gastly, and horrible" (367:8).

Not merely the conventional image of the dishonest tradesman prompted, therefore, Butler's characterization of the tailor as one who "Came in with the Curse; and is younger Brother unto Thorns, and Thistles, and Death" — a passage which continues by saying that, "if *Adam* had not fallen, he had never sat crossleg'd," and that "Sin and he [the tailor] are Partners" (p. 174). Clearly, in such references, the fashioning of clothes symbolizes the fallen condition of man — not only the *original error* caused by Adam's innocence, but also the perpetuation of the human tendency to deceive and be deceived that is occasioned by man's use of reason. Nevertheless, reason is, paradoxically, the only means by which error may be avoided and truth attained.

II *Human Nature*

This view of the paradoxical condition of "rational" man is the basis of Butler's theories of human nature and knowledge. Fallen mankind, he suggests, both in the notebook and, implicitly, in the prose *characters*, consists largely of knaves (those who employ reason to deceive others) and of the ignorant (those who are rationally deceived by knaves or by themselves). Fools and madmen comprise a third category of quasi-humanity: those creatures who — either through natural privation or accidental impairment (327:2) — lack the rational means of determining their proper places in the order of nature. Like the "natural" fool in Shakespeare's *King Lear*, the fools and madmen of this third group possess, Butler suggests, a special license (which the rationally endowed ignorant are denied) to pursue their delusions: "That Providence," he notes, "that Cloaths and Feede's Beasts, because they know not how to help themselves, Provides for all Sorts of Fooles, that are aequally incapable of Relieving themselves without it" (329:1). Moreover, what little wit a fool has "tends naturaly to knavery, and he is dishonest by instinct" (p. 275). Natural fools (and madmen), then, survive in a world where

reason is perverted into fraud, and where knavery becomes a
"rational" science — the "Mechanics of Cheat" and the "mathematical Magic of Imposture," as Butler calls it (p. 214). In the symbolic clothing of the church, the courts, the various trades, and, of
course, the underworld, such knavery appeals (often in extremely
subtle ways) to rational man's capacity for incomplete knowledge
and for self-approving "opinion" — to his *ignorance,* the word by
which Butler distinguishes fallen man's tendency to err from the
original folly that led an innocent Adam to believe he was God's
equal. Butler therefore regarded knavery as "a just Judgment, sent
into this World to punish the Confidence and Curiosity of
Ignorance, that out of a natural Inclination to Error will tempt its
own Punishment, and help to abuse itself" (p. 171).

But the ignorant also directly deceive themselves. Rejecting the
instruction of experience as prejudicial, such men have lost Eden for
nothing (343:4); and they remain, in spite of the divine direction to
study, observe, and practice, as liable to "venture beyond [their]
Latitude" as any fool or madman (288:1). The latter types, Butler
believed, are governed by the imagination, that "Sayle" of the understanding that is "apt to receive, and be carry'd away with every
winde of vanity, unles it be stear'd" by reason, its "only Helme"
(336:2). On the other hand, reason, which was given to man for self-
knowledge, will produce its own illusions unless it submit its conceptions to "the Judgment, and Arbitration of Sense" (363:2). Since
man's "natural affectation" [*sic*] for himself makes objective in-
trospection impossible (for "no Man can possibly be a Competent
Judge of his own Conceptions, unless he cou'd have more Reason
than he has" [274:5]), his only sure means to knowledge lies in exter-
nals — in the empirical evidence of natural order and of his own
place within that order. Wanting this recourse to the sensuous nature
of things, or, where that is unobtainable, to "collaterall Precedents,
and Paralels from such as may be" (363:2), reason produces not
truth, but "speculation," a word which Butler uses (cf. Lat.
speculum) in the sense of "mirror" (280:6); therefore, the "notions"
of the speculative reason reflect not nature (351:1) but the mind's
own desires (287:1). Without sense, Butler observed, reason is like a
glass eye "which though it cannot see, can make a Show as if it did,
and is proof against al those accidents that use to destroy true ones"
(333:2). For this reason, he believed, "al Ignorant People, are . . .
naturally obstinate, in all things which they believe they know, only
because they know nothing to the Contrary" (333:2).

To the partiality of such speculation, Butler traced much of the contentiousness of human learning. Theology that ignores the empirical evidence of "the Booke of Nature" and philosophy — both ancient and modern — are "speculative" in Butler's sense of the word. The philosopher described in his *characters* makes hypotheses "as a Taylor does a Doublet without Measure, no Matter whether they fit *Nature*, he can make *Nature* fit them" (p. 94). Aristotle, Butler noted elsewhere, studied nature "more in the metaphysiques of his own Braine, then her own certaine operations; As if his chiefest care had been to make his Systemes . . . agree among themselves very prettily, but perhaps without any great regard to Truth or Nature" (403:4). Democritus' mechanistic theory could have been "hit upon" only by one "mad enough to put out his owne eies" in order "that he might contemplate the better" (461:6); and the rationalist Descartes, whose distrust of both received philosophy and the delusive effects of sense led to his purging of all but self-evident truths from the mind, erred in believing the intellect "so cleare, and Infallible" that it did not require the "more Authenticall" test of sense (363:2).

But Butler's most elaborate illustration of the delusiveness of reason is made at the expense of seventeenth century science — in *The Elephant in the Moon*, one of several satires that Butler wrote about the Royal Society. Like Swift, Butler was critical of the impracticalities of modern science, its exhibitionism, and its apparent refusal to direct its own efforts by common sense standards of value. His general attitude toward such efforts may perhaps be deduced from the fact that he endowed Hudibras with scientific knowledge:

> . . . he by *Geometrick* scale
> Could take the size of *Pots of Ale;*
> Resolve by Sines and Tangents straight,
> If *Bread* or *Butter* wanted weight;
> And wisely tell what hour o'th' day
> The Clock does strike, by Algebra. (I, i, 121 - 26)

In the fragmentary "Satire on the Royal Society," Butler assembled a similar list of "occupations" for its members:

> To measure wind, and weigh the air,
> And turn a circle to a square;
> To make a powder of the Sun,
> By which all doctors should b' undone;

> To find the North-west passage out,
> Although the farthest way about. (ll. 87 - 92)

The end of true knowledge, Butler believed, was a simple and modest one: the understanding of "what is Fit to be don" (276:6), as he stated it in his notebook. "Things that ly far of[f] the Sense" need not be known at all, and nature adapted human vision accordingly (364:3). But developments in optical science had removed this natural safeguard, and opened to men a limitless sphere for worthless speculation and error.

The obvious joke of *The Elephant in the Moon* is that science makes mountains out of molehills: the virtuosos of a "Learn'd *Society*" make a lunar elephant out of a mouse. But more interesting than the theme of scientific error in the poem (Butler refers to the controversy over the validity of telescopic evidence waged in 1670 and 1671 by Joseph Glanvill and Henry Stubbe)[7] is Butler's concern with the general ethical issue of man's attitude toward falsehood and truth — specifically, with his use of reason to cultivate falsehood and to subvert truth in the interest of self-esteem. The poem describes the behavior of a group of virtuosi who one evening turn their telescope upon the moon — which they assume to be inhabited — and observe (or believe they observe) the inhabitants engaged in a war. Then,

> . . . a stranger Sight appears
> Than e're was seen in all the Spheres:
> An *Elephant* from one of those
> Two mighty Armies is broke loose,
> And with the Horrour of the Fight;
> Appears amaz'd, and in a Fright. (ll. 121 - 28)

In great excitement the observers agree "to draw an exact Narrative" of their observations; and, while they are engrossed in this work, the footboys take their turn at the telescope. With eyes unclouded by vanity or by learned hypotheses — with little more than "Monkey Ingenuity" — they promptly identify the lunar armies as "swarms of flies and gnats" and the elephant as a mouse that had "gotten in/The hollow tube" (ll. 353 - 54).

The poem presents, then, two "discoveries": an elephant on the moon, and a mouse in a telescope. The first discovery (together with the incorrect identification of insects as warring armies) is anticipated — the hypostatized end of a long sequence of nonsequiturs, circular reasonings, and deductions from invalid assumptions. Sensitive to the public ridicule of their past experiments, the virtuosi seize upon the notion of a lunar war as the means of improving the image of the society. No longer, says the chief spokesman for the group (Robert Boyle, perhaps),[8]

> . . . shall our ablest *Virtuosos*
> Prove Arguments for Coffee-houses;
> . . . .
> Nor shall our past Misfortunes more
> Be charg'd upon the ancient Score:
> . . . .
> This one Discovery's enough,
> To take all former Scandals off. (ll. 205 - 26)

The second discovery (that of the mouse, or truth) is resisted and is reasoned against by the members of the Royal Society; at one point, it is suggested that "the Cause of th' *Elephant, or Mouse"* be decided by ballot, that the virtuosos "find, or make, the Truth by Votes" (l. 476). When an earlier observation casts some doubt upon the existence of the elephant, each virtuoso is "Resolv'd . . . to make [the discovery] good . . . And rather his own Eyes condemn,/Than question what h' had seen with them" (ll. 257 - 60). But what had the virtuosos seen? The elephant is not a perception at all; it is a rational invention, a "speculation." Thus one of Butler's virtuosos triumphantly concludes that the existence of *"Elephants . . .* in the *Moon*/Though we had now discover'd none,/Is easily made manifest" (ll. 145 - 47).

The self-delusiveness of human nature is, of course, exaggerated for comic effect in *The Elephant in the Moon.* Nevertheless, though Butler stopped short of outright skepticism — which could itself be merely another mask of ignorance (286:3) — his distrust of intellectual efforts which serve to improve man's own and others' opinions of himself was genuine. Truth, he believed, exists — the standard by which man finds his place in the order of nature; but, as truth wants "that free latitude to flourish in, which error always usurpes" (293:4), men frequently avoid it. A more complete statement of this idea, together with the mythical implications we have been noticing, is made by another of the virtuosos (probably Robert Hooke) in *The Elephant in the Moon*. When the footboys innocently uncover the fact that the elephant is in truth a mouse, he remarks that

> . . . Truth is too reserv'd, and nice,
> T'appear in mix'd Societies;
> Delights in solit'ary Abodes,
> And never shews her self in Crowds;
> A sullen little Thing, below
> All Matters of Pretence and Show;
>
> . . . .
>
> For, what has Mankind gain'd by knowing
> His little Truth, but his Undoing,
> Which wisely was by Nature hidden,
> And only for his Good forbidden?
> And, therefore, with great Prudence does
> The World still strive to keep it close;
> For if all secret Truths were known,
> Who would not be once more undone?
> For Truth has always Danger in't,
> And here, perhaps, may cross some Hint,
> We have already agreed upon . . . (ll. 405 - 10; 419 - 29)

The speaker refers not only to the "Learn'd *Society*" of Butler's satire but to the society of all rational men who are united in the common effort to subvert the truth that threatens to strip them of their pretensions.

III *Poetry*

Butler's awareness of the human tendency to ignore truth which is unflattering was also an important factor in determining his theory of poetry: if men can tamper with their own consciences (as is implied in the final lines of the passage last quoted), it is doubtful that they will respect the truths offered by another — even when, as tradition held, that other was divinely inspired. However, Butler himself did not necessarily hold the poet in such esteem. His notebook makes few comments about poetry or its authors; and those we find — excepting an approving reference to Ben Jonson (398:6) — are generally adversely critical. He regarded verse as a counterfeit mode of expression — having *"something in the Stamp and Coyne, to answer for the Allay, and want of Intrinsique value"* — and, beliving it "harder to imitate Nature, then any Deviation from her," he argued that "Prose require's a more Proper and Natural Sense, and expression then verse" (408:6). Like Swift, Butler distrusted serious poetry, for he associated the flights of fancy (that in devoted circles were considered as "inspiration" or as wit) with religious enthusiasm and madness. His satirical *character* of "A Small Poet" employs the analogy of the *"Fanatic,* that inspires himself with his own Whimsies" (p. 82); and his notebook states that "Gifts and wit are but a kind of Hotheadednes, that Renders those that are Possest with it, better at Extempore, than Premeditation . . ." (452:1). The poet Sir John Denham's recovery from madness — which Butler celebrated in a mock "Panegyric" — provided the perfect opportunity to make the point:

> Sir, you've outlived so desperate a fit,
> As none could do, but an immortal wit;
> Had yours been less, all helps had been in vain,
> And thrown away, tho' on a less sick brain.
> But you were so far from receiving hurt,
> You grew improved, and much the better for't. (ll. 1 - 6, *P. W.*)

Butler subscribed to a conservative æsthetic that regarded true wit as the product of both judgment and fancy; judgment, as Hobbes declared, produced "the strength and structure"; fancy, "the Ornaments of a Poem."[9] The same point is made even more explicitly when Butler counsels men to "make Truth and observation the Ground and Foundation, or rather the end of their Studys, and use Fancy, and Stile only as Instrumentall, to express their Conceptions the more easily, and Naturally . . ." (340:2). Wit, he noted, was a "slight of the Minde" that "deliver's things otherwise then they are in Nature, by rendring them greater or lesse then they really are (which is cal'd Hyperbole) or by putting them into some other condition then Nature ever did (as when the Performances of Sensible, and Rationall Beings are apply'd to Senseles and Inanimate things, with which the writings of Poets abound)" (336:1).

It will readily be seen that the "slight of Minde" to which Butler likened wit is similar to that human tendency toward deception that he frequently decried in his notebook. Indeed, although it was probably already a convention by Butler's time, clothing — his symbol of the means of that deception — is a common analogy for wit in his writing. Hudibras, we read, seemed "loath to wear . . . out" his wit; therefore, he used it only "on Holy-dayes, or so,/As men their best Apparel do" (I, i, 47 - 50). The "Small Poet" of the *characters* is described as a "Haberdasher" who makes the most of his "very small Stock" of wit through thrift, theft, and rhetorical substitutes (p. 82). Writers who are given to obscurities of style are likened to "Citizens that commonly choose the Darkest streets to set up in, or make false lights that the Spots and Steines of their Stuffs may not be perceived" (402:5). Just as fallen man uses reason to create a false paradise, the poet often uses wit to project a vanished Golden Age upon the present Age of Iron: he converts men into heroes and women into nymphs (p. 86). Thus the virtuosos in *The Elephant in the Moon* attempt to narrow the credibility gap created in their hoax by calling upon one,

> . . . who for his Excellence
> In height'ning Words and shad'wing Sense,
> And magnifying all he writ
> With curious microscopic Wit,
> Was magnify'd himself no less. (ll. 167 - 71)

Butler did not, however, condemn all wit; "when it imploys those things which it borrows of Falshood, to the Benefit and advantage of Truth, as in Allegories, Fables, and Apologues, it is of excellent use," he believed, "as making a Deeper impression into the mindes of Men then if the same Truths were plainely deliver'd" (336:1), for wit has the power of raising the passions and of short-circuiting reason and judgment to excite the will directly (336:2). Moreover, since wit is "capable of Prodigie and strangnes, and of neare kin to a Ly which . . . [men] have ever been naturally inclynd to," it is a better means of teaching moral truths than either reason or precept (282:1). Even in political action, Butler recognized the advantages of wit over reason. The "chiefest Art of Government," he noted, was the ability "to convert the Ignorance, Folly, and Madness of Mankinde . . . to their own good, which can never be don, by telling them Truth and Reason . . . but by little Tricks and Devises (as they cure Mad men) . . ." (391:1). The poet too, if he employs wit "to the Benefit and advantage of Truth" (i.e., if he uses fancy to clothe the truth), may, we should conclude, be able to deceive men for their own good.

Though Butler's conception of fancy as a mere instrument for expressing truth is a critical commonplace of neo-Classicism, little else in his critical pronouncements justifies this label. That stubborn adherence to the facts of experience that prevented his endorsing the theoretical justification of rational man tended also to invalidate any rational system for judging literature. The *Nature* exalted in neo-Classical criticism was, in part at least, the Aristotelian Nature which moved always away from accidents and toward perfection. Such a view did not ignore empirical reality — the accidental world of phenomena — but its preference for intellectually conceived perfection is clearly apparent in the doctrine of poetic kinds which sanctioned realism only at a specified distance from the more respected forms of tragedy and epic. But, for Butler, the "truths" that his age found embodied in the heroic fictions of the higher genres were flattering ameliorations that contradicted the picture of man and his world acquired through sense and experience. To Butler, the modern writer of romance who follows the practice of the ancient heroic poets "Pulls down old Histories to build them up finer again, after a new Model of his own designing," and he "takes away all the Lights of Truth in History to make it the fitter Tutoress of Life" (p. 169). There remains only one decorum of practical value to the modern writer of heroics, Butler ironically concludes: "He observes one very fit Decorum in dating his Histories in the Days of old, and putting all his own Inventions upon ancient Times; for when the World was younger, it might, perhaps, love, and fight, and do generous Things at the Rate he describes them; but since it is grown old, all these heroic Feats are laid by and utterly given over, nor ever like to come in fashion again" (p. 169). The decorum of heroic literature, the suiting of a grand style to a great subject, merely conceals the essential inconsistency of human nature.

A similar criticism is made of the Classical decorum of tragedy, which, from Butler's point of view, also affirmed a morality that could only appear arbitrary when judged by the circumstances of real life. One of the specific targets in Butler's satire "Upon Critics Who Judge of Modern Plays Precisely by the Rules of the Ancients" — a general attack upon the abstract morality of Thomas Rymer's *Tragedies of the Last Age* (1678) — was Aristotle's prescription that tragedy arouse both pity and fear in the spectator, and (since pity is generated by undeserved misfortune and fear by the misfortune of those like ourselves) that the tragic protagonist be neither eminently evil nor eminently good. Grounding his own views in experience, Butler believed, however, that "no Affliction can terrify others from the like, but where it is Justly Deservd," just as "none can move

Compassion that is not Injustly incurd" — neither of these effects
being possible in Aristotle's characters of "middling sizes" (451:1).
In other words, the Aristotelian rules governing plot and character
destroy what Butler regarded as the didactic design of the dramatic
fable:

> No longer shall Dramatics be confined
> To draw true images of all mankind;
> To punish in effigy criminals,
> Reprieve the innocent, and hang the false;
> But a club-law to execute and kill,
> For nothing, whomsoe'er they please, at will,
> To terrify spectators from committing
> The crimes they did, and suffer'd for, unwitting. (ll. 51 - 58, *P. W.*)

In Rymer's rules of correctness, Butler saw another instance of the
deceptiveness of reason unqualified by the senses or, in this case, by
feeling. Rymer, he believed, allowed his head to rule his heart; he
tried to judge — as the title of Butler's satire "Upon Critics" puts it
— "*Precisely* by the Rules of the Ancients," using as it were an instrument of science — "cylinders of Torricellian glasses" (a baro-
meter) — to measure "the air upon Parnassus" (ll. 15 - 16). What
was inimical to reason (the imagination), Rymer ignored.

For Butler, such a critical system gave the neo-Classical poet only
a new appearance of value. The modern critic could well afford to
scoff at the Elizabethan pose of imaginative inspiration when the
scientific climate of the new age made rational control an even more
acceptable counterfeit for true poetry. Judging literature purely on
the strength of its effectiveness, Butler was aware of both forms of
poetic pretense; he could ridicule the new rhetorical wit of antithesis
as well as the stylistic excess of the Metaphysicals: the latter, he
remarks in the *character* of "A Quibbler," "is already cried down,
and the other . . . the only Elegance of our modern Poets . . . having
nothing in it but *Easiness,* and being never used by any lasting Wit,
will in wiser Times fall to nothing of itself" (p. 133).

What most sharply differentiates Butler's views on literature from
those of the neo-Classicists is this resistance to critical theory. Alexander Pope, for example, was able to reconcile the differences
between poetic truth and real knowledge; for, to Pope, though "wit
and judgment often are at strife," they are "meant [to be] each
other's aid," as he wrote in *The Essay on Criticism,* "like man and
wife." Pope implies that in the best literary practice wit and justice

are in fact reconciled. Those *"nameless Graces"* that lie "beyond the Reach of Art" do not invalidate his system; they simply stand outside it. For Butler, however, no such accommodation was possible: though "there is no tru wit that is not produc'd by a great Deal of Judgment," wit (or imagination) and reason (or judgment) "will [n]ever be brought to stand in Tune together" (328:2). True wit is always mysterious; there is no rational justification for it: the best wits, Butler notes, "have just confidence enough to keep them from utterly Renouncing" their wit, "which they are apt to do upon the smallest Check, if something else then their own Inclination did not oppose them in it" (326:1). This confidence (just sufficient, we should note), he regarded as the true "Poeticall Fury" (330:1); and it was to be found, significantly, not in the heroic but in the comic genres — particularly in satire. In fact, Butler completely inverted the traditional hierarchy of poetic kinds by setting above the heroic poem even the often judiciously condemned lampoon which, "if rightly considered," is "capable of doing Princes more good [than flattering panegyric] . . . and like Charmes easily Cure those Fantastique Distempers in Governments, which being neglected grow too stubborn to obey any but as Rigid Medecines" (431:5).

The "something else" that opposes the satirist's judgment is his anger, an emotion aroused by the folly and ignorance of the world. "It is difficult not to write satire," Juvenal wrote in his first satire; and Butler noted from the same source that "nothing . . . provokes and Sharpens wit like Malice, and Anger" (330:1). But the satirist manages to avoid the imaginative irresponsibility of excessive passion by virtue of the fact that his poetic images of folly and ignorance are essentially consistent with reality. Unlike the heroic poet, who is transported by a rapture of love for "what should be" — that other "Kinde of Fooles Paradise" that is actually beneficial to folly and knavery (276:1) — the comic poet and satirist (Butler makes little distinction between the two) are imaginatively transported by a rapture of hatred for "what is." Satires, therefore, "that are only provok'd with the Madnes and Folly of the world, are found to conteine more wit, and Ingenuity then all other writings whatsoever, and meet with a better Reception from the world, that is always more delighted to heare the Faults and vices though of itself well describd, then all the Panegyriques that ever were" (330:1). For, whereas "Heroicall Poetry handle's the slightest, and most Impertinent Follys in the world in a formall Serious and unnaturall way," comedy, burlesque, and satire handle "the most Serious [matters] in a Frolique and Gay humor which has always been found the more apt to instruct, and instill those Truths with Delight into men, which they would not indure to heare of any other way" (278:3).

Experience had taught Butler that in real men the traditional attributes of literary greatness disguised qualities quite the reverse of those to which they were attached in the tragedy and in the epic. Like Falstaff, Butler regarded the heroic ideal of honor as "a mere scutcheon," as an empty term peddled by heralds (p. 116) and claimed by highwaymen (p. 279). At best, this term designated "a mere Negative Continence," as of women "only not being whores" (341:5). More frequently, Butler associated heroic honor with the stubbornness of the ignorant. Under the rubric "Opinion" in the notebook, he wrote that "men of Honor are in Probability the most like to take the worst courses (if no other will serve) to vindicate that Reputation, the Loss of which is so grievious to them, and the shame so Intollerable" (351:2). In the notebook and in the *characters*, the romantic images of honor are common analogies for the deception of self and others. Butler notes that the fashion of witty repartee is a "modern way of Running at Tilt," in which victory depends upon "Confidence" (arrogant self-conceit) as formerly it depended upon "the best Beaver" (470:5). His modern knights-errant may be found in the mock-Pindarick on "the Most Renouned Du-Vall" (a highwayman), and in such *characters* as the "Hector" (p. 278), the "Anabaptist" (p. 215), the "Mountebank" (p. 181), and the "Opiniater," who, like the ignorant man, is pledged "by his Order to defend the weak and distressed" by delivering "enchanted Paradoxes" and obscurities from "invisible Castles" (p. 220). No doubt recent history also contributed to the bankruptcy of the heroic ideal, for although "no Age ever abounded more with Heroical Poetry then the present . . . yet there was never any wherein fewer Heroicall Actions were performd" (442:1). Butler had witnessed "two living burlesques," Ricardo Quintana has said: for "what had the Commonwealth been but a romance . . . And if recent poets were to be believed, what was the Restoration period but an epic?"[10] Butler's note on the Long Parliament demonstrates one half of this view: "The Long Parliament to secure the Liberties of the People from themselves, hid them in the invisible Hands of those Fayries the keepers of the Libertys. But Oliver stormd the Inchanted Castle, and tooke the Lady into his own Protection" (433:1).

In a world in which the traditional images of heroism can become disguises of falsehood, the disenchanting satirist is the true hero. "A

Satyr," Butler wrote, "is a kinde of Knight Errant that goe's upon Adventures, to Relieve the Distressed Damsel Virtue, and Redeeme Honor out of Inchanted Castles, And opprest Truth, and Reason out of the Captivity of Gyants or Magitians . . ." (469:2). Such a knight enjoys none of the glamor of his literary prototype: indeed, the preceding passage goes on to say that the satirist "has enough to do to secure himselfe against the Penaltys of Scandalum Magnatum, and Libells." His realm is the real world; his task, the exposure of the fallen human condition that is often revealed in his own weakness and imperfection. The "Satyr" as knight is thus an emblem of the lowly, inelegant hudibrastic burlesque; of *Hudibras* (the poem. not the character); and of Butler's conception of true wit: disguise that makes us see what is otherwise concealed.

IV *Some Specific Views*

Thus far, what we have been calling "Butler's thought" is for the most part a set of assumptions which underlies his frequently inconsistent reflections on knowledge, man, and literature that are recorded in his notebook and, after witty refinement, in his prose *characters* and verse satires. The same body of writing (together with a large number of verse fragments on various subjects — the "Poetical Thesarus" in Lamar's edition of the minor verse — and the prose notes in the manuscript commonplace book) also contains many expressions of opinion about more specific matters. In the preceding pages, we have drawn indiscriminately from the thirteen general categories in which Butler arranged his prose reflections in the British Museum manuscript. His thinking on two more of these subjects — "Government" and "Religion" — deserve our attention yet.

Coloring Butler's opinions on both these subjects is his frank acknowledgement of the chaotic state of the world of human affairs. Disorder is real, he believed, and it is here to stay. Democracy is "the effect of a crazy brain," he wrote in the *character* of "A Republican" (p. 59); and political theorists, like James Harrington and his fellow members of the Rota, are impractical dreamers; for, believers in words rather than things, they are unable to "understand the Difference between Speculation and Practice" (p. 56). Even more concrete efforts to improve social institutions through political revolution or through religious reformation were, he believed, certain to fail. The futility of such action, Butler seems to have felt, is due to the impossibility of rational appeal — of reducing (as Swift put it in *A Tale of a Tub*) the notions of every member of society "exactly to the same Length, and Breadth, and Height" as that of the reformer, who must therefore use unjust means to achieve his ends. (Butler, like Swift, also observed the one exception to this rule: that if a madman "have the Luck to meet with many of [his] own temper, instead of being ridiculous, [he] becomes a Church" [p. 190]).

Thus, Butler maintained, rebellion is promoted "with nothing else but Lyes, and cheates and Impostures. For civil Armes can neither be raysd, nor maintained, by honest meanes" (302:7). And, at another place, he contradicts the Hobbesian notion that a de facto government is a government de jure by observing that "an unjust Title [to a seat of government] cannot be supported but by unjust meanes. And for want of this all our late usurpations miscarrid" (383:1). In other words, an unjust ruler must become a tyrant to maintain himself; and tyranny only incites further revolution. But this conclusion is a political fact that even princes with a just title to rule must recognize, none of whom, Butler maintained, "would deny his Subjects Liberty of Conscience if it were in his Power to grant it, without violating the Law of selve-preservation; for it being the Nature of all Sects (like other vermine) to increase and multiply, there is no Religion that can become the most Numerous but do's Naturally incline to suppress or destroy all others, and to give way to that, is to take part with such as indeavour to subvert the Government" (429:4). Should a king, then, tyrannically oppose the forces of civil disorder, and run the risk of arousing open rebellion, or should he grant his subjects the liberty they crave and, in effect, voluntarily license the subversion of his government? How is political order to be maintained?

Butler's answer to this question is interesting. In one of the verse fragments in the notebook he writes:

> when a Nation is a Slave,
> What Crowns of Monarchs can be safe?
> And still the less we wast [demand] our Right
> W' Injoy the greater Freedom by't.[11]

Thus, Butler would have advised the king to govern tyrannically — at least during the infancy of his state; "for as that which was Tyranny at first do's in time become Liberty, So there is no Liberty but in the beginning was Tyranny. All unripe fruite is harsh . . ." (382:1).

The concluding analogy, one of several to the processes of natural evolution in this passage, adumbrates a theory of government as organism: "Governments like Natural Bodys have their times of growing Perfection and Declining, and according to their Constitutions, some hold out longer, and some decay sooner then other, but all in their beginings and infancies are subject to . . . many Infirmities and Imperfections . . . Governments are made like Naturall Productions by Degrees according as their Materials are brought in by time, and those Parts of it that are unagreeable to their Nature, cast of[f]." (382:1) And, in the *character* of "A Republican," Butler makes the point even more clearly: "he forgets that no Government was ever made by model: For they are not built as Houses are, but grow as Trees do. And as some Trees thrive best in one Soil, some in another; so do Governments, but none equally in any, but all generally where they are most naturally produced" (p. 56).

Butler's conception of government as a dynamic and changing organism — his rejection of the notion of a state as a static and inanimate structure that may be constructed from a blueprint — is another illustration of his distance from the more Humanist stance of Augustan thinkers. For them, nature was, in one sense, itself a grand blueprint or, in another sense, the "fabric" realized from that plan. Locke referred to the Deity as an "Architect," and Johnson spoke of the art of the mason as "one of the principal arts by which reasoning beings are distinguished from the brute" (*Adventurer*, 128). For such men, as Paul Fussell has pointed out, the contrast between the natural and the artificial, the animate and the inanimate, was felt as a difference between "the temporary and the permanent, the frail and the powerful, the puny and the majestic, the living thing that crawls the earth and the cold, lifeless thing that triumphs over gravitation and time."[12] Butler would have felt that such an attitude failed to account for the dynamics of human society, the *accidents* in nature that contradicted even God's plan. In human affairs, it was the artificial, the abstract, and the inanimate that broke down. The mechanistic analogy used by Descartes to describe the mind, and by Hobbes to describe the state, served Butler only as a metaphor of folly and ignorance. But as an organism, the state was to Butler both susceptible to illness and able to restore itself to health and vigor. Permitted to develop naturally — without the revolutions of disgruntled elements in society, or the impositions of reforming theorists — a tyrannical state will gradually adapt itself to the real conditions in which it must exist. Butler very likely regarded the constitutional monarchy of the Restoration as such an evolving organism, for "among Governments," he noted, "Monarchy has in the manage and practice of it more of Commonwealth, and Commonwealth more of Monarchy then either have of what they are cald. For noe Monarch can possibly Governe alone, but must of Necessity submit and be ruled by the advice, and Counsell of others" (437:1). And in this connection, he observed that "there is nothing in Nature more Arbitrary than a Parliament, and yet there is nothing Else that is able to preserve the Nation from being Govern'd by an Arbitrary Power — and confine Authority within a Limited Compass" (273:7). Quite literally, Butler's political philosophy was a science of dealing with the imperfect.

To this view of government as an organism may also be traced Butler's anti-Catholic and anti-Puritan positions, which are in large part political. The threat of Catholicizing England (of which he complains much more bitterly than of the Puritanizing of the nation) represented to him the transplanting of foreign stock that was unnatural to the native climate and soil: the promoting of "the Interests *of a foreign Prince; in opposition to o*ʳ owne," and the removing of "the Staples of Religion, so well settled heere, *into the dominions of fforreiners.*"[13] Popery, "having serv'd out an Apprenticeship to Tyranny, [and] as soon as it was out of its time . . . set up for itself" (273:8), had evolved as a form of tyranny "most advantagious . . . to weake Princes."[14] Butler implies that the post-Reformation soil of England would reject the Roman transplant with all the consequent upheaval of a new reformation. Puritanism, on the other hand, quite obviously constituted an interruption of the natural evolution of English government. If Butler found the best features of a commonwealth in monarchy, he found the worst features of monarchy in the Puritan commonwealth: "in the Senates of Republiques Some one Commonly governes all the rest, and has that really in power, which Princes have but in Name" (438). Indeed, Butler saw little difference between Catholic tyranny and Puritan tyranny.

Butler also considered the Catholic and the Puritan as theological (or, better, *psychological*) brethren — an illustration of his assumption that extremes meet. The ground of his criticism here was the irrationality of these religions — no real inconsistency with his criticism of the unaided use of abstract reason implicit in his ethical and intellectual views. At any rate, his insistence upon a reasonable basis for faith is one of the few unequivocal positions he takes in his observations about religion, which are virtually impossible to reduce to the tenets of a recognizable denomination: "Faith can determine nothing of Reason, but Reason can of Faith, and therefore if Faith be above Reason, (as some will have it) it must be reason only that can make it appear to be so . . . Faith cannot define Reason, but Reason can Faith, and therefore it should seeme to be the lardger" (338:1).

Such a statement does not, of course, make Butler a Deist; for seventeenth century Anglicanism had rationalist as well as fideist adherents.[15] On the other hand, those marginal references, in his manuscript commonplace book, to seventeenth century English churchmen — references which suggest to Norma Bentley that possibly "toward the end of his life Butler found the Church of England more satisfying" — may, as Hugh de Quehen even more plausibly suggests, be the notations of the manuscript's transcriber, William Longueville.[16] If Butler was a Deist, he was one who believed in the divinity of Christ: "Hoc est Corpus meum, is true in a Litteral Sense," he writes in his notebook, "for as Bread naturally turnes to Flesh, and wine to bloud; He, to whom all times are present might very properly say that is, that was to bee" (302:1).

But Butler's Christianity rested upon the broadest possible basis: since "all men agree in the end of Religion that God is to be worshiped" (299:2), "let all bee done out of *that only true Principle* of obedience; Love to God; presented vnto Him upon *that only ground of Acceptation*, Jesus Christ; & seasoned wth that Acceptable Grace, Humility."[17] The point is that Butler was not interested in the doctrinal opinions that account for denominational distinctions; nor did he believe that God was interested in them any "further then they conduce to . . . [men's] own Peace and Quietnes" (433:4).

CHAPTER 3

Hudibras

I *History*

BUTLER described the genesis of the first part of *Hudibras* in his letter of March 19, 1662/3, to Sir George Oxenden. He had become acquainted, he wrote, with "a West Countrey Kn^t then a Coll: in the Parliament Army & a Com^te man" who had lodged in the same house with him in Holbourne; and, finding "his humor soe pleasant," he endeavored (almost fortuitously, he suggests) "to render his Character as like as I could."[1] Sir Hudibras' squire, Ralph, was modeled on a clerk employed by Butler's fellow lodger. This employee, Butler continues in the letter, was "an Independ^t, betweene whome, & ye Kn^t, there fell out Such perpetuall disputes about Religion, as you will find up & downe in ye Booke for as neere as I could I sett downe theire very words. As for ye Story I had it from ye Kn^ts owne Mouth, & is so farr from being feign'd, y^t it is upon Record, for there was a Svite of Law upon it betweene ye Kn^t, & ye Fidler, in wch ye K^nt was overthrowne to his great shame, & discontent, for wch he left ye Countrey & came up to Settle at London." Butler, who denied any deeper level of historical reference in the poem, remarked that his "chiefe designe was onely to give ye world a Just Acco^t of ye Ridiculous folly & Knavery of ye Presbiterian & Independent Factions then in power. . . ."

We have no reason to doubt Butler's statement that *Hudibras* was originally conceived as a comic retelling of an actual court action brought about by an overzealous Presbyterian magistrate against an overexuberant merrymaker (overexuberant at least by Puritan standards), for the narrative is interspersed with the pretentious theological haggling between the magistrate and his Independent clerk. If such a motivating incident seems rather trivial, we need only recall Parliament's closing of the theaters and its curtailment of public amusements in 1642 and 1647 to find historical precedent. Moreover, the exaggeration of the trivial — a means of inflating one's own importance and of diverting attention from one's own real faults — was a quirk of human nature that frequently attracted Butler's satiric attention. The Puritans themselves conceived of their zeal for piety — the special gift of God to a chosen few — as a sort of romantic *gloire*, and they practiced and cultivated it with all the seriousness that a Medieval knight dedicated to his chivalric calling. Butler merely had to exploit the comic possibilities in these materials, to portray his West Country magistrate and the clerk as a latter-day Don Quixote and Sancho Panza, and to depict their legal entanglement with a fiddler as a Puritan-tilting-at-windmills — inspired, however, by self-interested materialism rather than by idealism. Butler renamed his hero Hudibras, after the "sterne melancholy" lover of Perissa's eldest sister in Spenser's *Faerie Queene*, a knight "not so good of deedes, as great of name . . . more huge in strength, than wise in workes" (II, ii, 17) and one whose effort to make "peace is but continuall iarre" (II, ii, 26).[2] To his squire, Butler gave the name of Ralph or — depending on poetic exigencies — Ralpho or Raph, perhaps after the hero of Beaumont's *Knight of the Burning Pestle;*[3] and, to the original "story" of the knight and the fiddler, he supplied (if they were not a part of the original incident) a company "such as Commonly make up Bearebaitings."[4]

Of course Cervantes' ridicule of romance postures in *Don Quixote* (which was first translated into English in 1612 and 1620) and Beaumont's good-natured satire of middle class pretensions in *The Knight of the Burning Pestle* contributed more than the names of Butler's two protagonists. Quixote; his squire, Sancho Panza; and his mistress, Dulcinea de Toboso are all mentioned in *Hudibras* (I, ii, 310, 873; II, i, 876), and very likely one or two incidents in the poem (e.g., the whipping and the skimmington episodes of Part II) were suggested by the Spanish novel. The idea of deriving the names of the bear-baiters from their occupations was probably suggested by the occurrence of the device in Beaumont's play. No doubt other works significantly stimulated Butler's invention: for example, Rabelais' *Gargantua and Pantagruel*, on matters of law, learning, and women; and we know from one of Butler's notes to the first part of the poem (i, 639 - 40) that he was acquainted with Paul Scarron's French burlesque, *Virgile Travesti*. Such matters are largely academic, however, and need not detain us here.[5] Whatever faults we may find in *Hudibras*, lack of originality is not one of them.

Finally, we should recognize that Butler's handling of the quarrels between the knight and his squire seems designed to suggest the uneasy alliance of Presbyterians and Independents within the general party of Puritans, the Protestant *purifiers* of the church. Historically, as in Butler's poem, the differences between these religious viewpoints arose over questions of church government. The Presbyterian scheme of ecclesiastical reform replaced the rule of bishops in the Anglican Church with a complex hierarchy of authority, a system in which individual congregations were governed by Presbyters, a number of congregations by a Classical Assembly or Classis, the Classes by a Provincial Synod, and the entire structure by a National Synod. The Independents, on the other hand, tolerated no authority over individual congregations; and, as indicated by Ralph in the first canto of the poem, they regarded the terms *"Provincial, Classick, National* [as] Mere humane Creature-cobwebs all"* (I, i, 807 - 08), and as no more lawful than a bear-baiting. The Independent derived his authority from a "liberty of conscience" and from a private "light" which guided him in matters of religion; and these assumptions the more conservative Presbyterians regarded as a license for dangerous innovation. Relations between Presbyterians and Independents were also strained by the fact that the Independents became a powerful force in Cromwell's army and that they had gained by 1647 political ascendency over the Presbyterians. Butler alludes to this power shift in the scene in which Hudibras, after trying to force Ralph to serve as his proxy in a whipping, is warned by his squire to remember "how in *Arms* and *Politicks*" the Independents have triumphed over the "holy Tricks" of Hudibras' party:

> Trepan'd your Party with *Intregue,*
> And took your *Grandees* down a peg.
> *New-modell'd* th' *Army,* and *Cashir'd*
> All that to *Legion-SMEC* adher'd,
> Made a mere Utensill o' your *Church,*
> And after left it in the lurch
> A Scaffold to build up our own,
> And when w' had done with't, pul'd it down. (II, ii, 519 - 28)

Butler's typical Presbyterian is — in the poet's own sense of the phrase — an ignorant fool; he is encumbered with the commonplaces of learning, the formal apparatus of logic and rhetoric, and the outmoded rituals of religion and knighthood. Butler's

Independent is a knave, a realist able both to penetrate rational deception and to deceive others with his own reason. Like his Independent prototype, the squire is a better fighter and, though he pretends to be a mystic, a more skillful reasoner than the Presbyterian knight. In battle, the squire's superiority lies in his practical knowledge of when to press an advantage and when to retreat; and, in an argument, he gets the better of Hudibras first by attacking the reality of words and then by arguing that words are the best weapons of war. This apparent inconsistency is not merely an expression of Butler's ambivalent attitude toward reason,[6] but also an effective expression of the unprincipled opportunism of the Independent and his party. We might notice in this connection Butler's comment in his notebook about the relationship between Don Quixote and Sancho Panza, the general models for his own knight and squire: ". . . the Author of Don Quixote, makes Sancho (though a Natural Fool) much more wise and Politique then his Master with all his Study'd, and acquir'd abilities" (327:2).

Although it is impossible to say whether Butler expected the characters and the actions of his poem to bear any additional allegorical significance than that mentioned in his letter to Oxenden, few readers have been able to resist extending this function in their interpretations of the poem. Even in Butler's own day, as he indicated in the letter, ". . . some curious witts heere pretend to discouer ceartaine Psons of Quality wth whome they say those Characters agree, but since I doe not know who they are I cannot tell you till I see theire Commentaries but am content (since I cannot helpe it) y'every man should make what applications he pleases of it, either to himselfe or others."[7] Many of these *discoveries* or identifications were to appear in an "Alphabetical Key to Hudibras," which has been ascribed to Sir Roger L'Estrange (1616 - 1704); and, though said to have been written "many Years since," this work was first published in the *Posthumous Works* (1715). Specifically, the "Key" attempts to supply the historical originals of Butler's characters: Hudibras is Sir Samuel Luke; Ralph, Isaac Robinson, "a zealous Botcher in *Moorfields*, who . . . was always contriving some new Quirpocut of Church-Government"; Crowdero, "one *Jackson* a Milliner in the *New-Exchange*," who took up fiddle playing in taverns after losing a leg in the service of the Roundheads; and the widow is "the precious Relique of *Aminadab Wilmot*, an Independent, kill'd at the Fight of *Edgehill*; and having Two-hundred Pounds *per Annum* left her for a Jointure."[8]

More recently, Hardin Craig, who has traced the "dim outlines of a political allegory" in Part I of *Hudibras*, states that "the brave resistance of the bear, his flight and establishment in a place of at least temporary comfort" suggest "the flight of King Charles from Hampton Court to Carisbrook," and that the knight's defeat by the bear-baiters suggests "the defeat of the Presbyterians and their overthrow by the leaders of the army."[9] Though it rather naturally follows from such an interpretation that Bruin, the bear in the poem, stands for Charles (and, with a bit more interpretive pressure, that the butcher Talgol stands for the Puritan commander Fairfax, and the "hard hostler" Colon for Cromwell), Craig, whose primary interest is in dating the composition of the poem, does not insist upon such identifications.

For W. S. Miller, however, the allegory of *Hudibras* is far too detailed for Butler to have been unaware of what he was accomplishing. Miller not only finds Butler's anti-Puritan sentiments objectified in Hudibras and in Ralph, but also uncovers vestiges of the poet's pre-Restoration anti-Royalism in the poem. "It is not unlikely," he writes, "that *Hudibras* took shape . . . from ambivalent feelings — anti-Presbyterian and anti-Independent, but nevertheless incorporating symbolic values for the king and for Cavalier forces that the Restoration would not tolerate."[10] If, as Miller assumes, Part I was taking shape in the 1640's when Butler was feeling little sympathy with a king "who had often flouted the British constitution," then, he argues, Talgol, Bruin, Trulla, and Magnano "certainly" appear as "Royalist symbols of some sort." Rather than recast these characters as Puritans after Charles' restoration, Butler merely strengthened "the anti-Puritan exterior" of the poem, taking refuge in the obscurity that "he was quite capable of achieving without the will to do so."[11] The immense success of *Hudibras* in the Restoration rested, then, upon a misinterpretation of the poem — one which Mr. Miller would have us believe Butler himself could have sanctioned, if not willed.

Actually, the temporal dimensions of *Hudibras* are even more complex than Miller believes. As John Wilders has shown, there are three demonstrable time levels in the poem: one "on which the characters look back in retrospect" (from 1640 to 1647); a second "in which Butler visualized the action of his poem as taking place" (between the end of 1647 and the end of 1648); and a third "during which he actually wrote" the major portion of Part I (between December 1653 and September 1658).[12] Nevertheless, Miller's hypothesis of an equally complex allegory must, when we remember Butler's views on politics and poetry, appear improbable; for the following statement can hardly be regarded as the sentiment of a Parliament man: "Princes ought to give their Subjects as much of the Shadow of Liberty as they can for their lives, but as little of the Reality of it, if they regard the Safety of themselves or their People" (383:2). Moreover, Butler, as we will recall, said "the less we wast our Right [to be other than slaves to a King] W' Injoy the greater Freedom by't." It is true that the imaginary world of *Hudibras* seems frequently about to verge upon the historical outlines of the real world of Commonwealth England. We should consider, for example, the political overtones in Butler's explanation of how Crowdero, the fiddler, lost his leg (an allusion to a Staffordshire folk tradition of crowning a king of musicians): "He bravely vent'ring at a Crown,/By chance of War was beaten down" (I, ii, 139 - 40). Or we have the passage describing Hudibras' riding out upon his first adventure:

> So have I seen with armed heel,
> A Wight bestride a *Common-weal;*
> While still the more he kick'd and spurr'd,
> The less the sullen Jade has stirr'd. (I, i, 917 - 20)

And, in this connection, we might notice that Miller's citation of lines from a contemporary ballad on the Long Parliament is both apposite and enlightening:

> Will you buy the Rumps great saddle,
>   With which it jockey'd the nation?
> And here is the bit and the bridle,
>   And curb of Dissimulation . . .[13]

Lines in the portrait of the astrologer Sidrophel call to mind the features of William Lilly and Sir Paul Neile; and Hudibras' wooing of the widow is suggestive of the attempts of the Puritans to become the lords of "Dame Religion" or of England herself.

But, beside these passages of oblique suggestiveness, we must place others which intrude upon the world of the poem with direct reference to the real world — negating, so it were, the reason for its allegory. If Hudibras' battle with the bear-baiters was meant to represent English politics in the 1640's, why should Butler have bothered to summarize explicitly the Puritan struggles of the same

period in the knight's harangue to the rabble (I, ii, 493 - 682)? Or, if
Hudibras' attempt to break his vow to the widow in Part II
represents allegorically the duplicity of the Puritan movement in
England, why is the point again made directly, as in the following?

> Did not our *Worthies* of the *House*,
> Before they broke the *Peace*, break *Vows?*
> For having free'd us, first from both
> Th' *Allegeance*, and *Supremacy-Oath;*
> Did they not, next, compel the *Nation*,
> To take, and break the *Protestation?* (ii, 149 - 54)

Such passages suggest that the historical allegory in *Hudibras* is at
best sporadic — improvisational, like the more local effects of wit in
the poem. When his satiric invention suggested the features of
reality, Butler eagerly seized upon and developed the resemblance;
but his invention was not determined by the data of history, nor
would he invent a witty resemblance to such data merely for its own
sake. Resemblances of the first sort reveal and intensify identity, il-
luminating and enlivening the literary image with recognitions of
reality; allegory of the second sort — "continued Allegory, or darke
conceit," as Spenser identified it — conceals identity, either
deliberately, or by making the act of recognition a gratuitous intellectual exercise.

We noticed in the preceding chapter Butler's interest in metaphor
and allegory as a means of deceiving men for their own good; but he
clearly disapproved of the use of allegory for such purposes of con-
cealment as Miller attributes to *Hudibras*. "Allegories are only
usefull," Butler observed in his notebook, "when they serve as
Instances, to illustrate Some obscure Truth": "But when a Truth,
Plaine enough, is forced to serve an Allegory, it is a prepostorous
mistake of the end of it; which is to make obscure things Plaine, not
Plaine things obscure . . . beside the Prepostorous Difficulty of forc-
ing things against their Naturall inclinations, which at the best do's
but discover how much wit a man may have to no purpose; there being no such Argument of a slight minde as an elaborate Triffle
(397:4). Finally, Butler believed that, although wit may be
prompted by individuals, it performs its true function only when it
sheds light on general human nature; for "wit is like Science not of
particulars, but universals," and "Arguments drawn from Particulars
signify little to universal Nature, which is the Proper object of
Science" (278:2).

II   *Satire*

In view of this criticism of allegory as a "dark conceit," it seems probable that Butler would have been less likely to write such an "elaborate Triffle" himself than to parody it or to ridicule the type of mind that produces it. This is not to say, of course, that *Hudibras* is a parody of the allegorical mode — although a passage like that in which Ralph proves that "*Synods* are mystical *Bear-gardens*" (I, ii, 1095 - 1250) might be read in this light. But, in another way, the poem is much concerned with trifles and with those who elaborate upon them. Two examples immediately come to mind: first, the moral scruple of the pharisaical Puritan whose conscience, Butler wrote in the *character* of "A Hypocritical Nonconformist," is so "taken up with such slight and little Matters, that it is impossible, it should ever be at Leisure to consider Things of greater Weight and Importance" (p. 47); and, second, the ceremonious conventions celebrated in heroic romance, the branch of literature which, Butler noted, "handle's the slightest, and most Impertinent Follys in the world in a formall Serious and unnaturall way" (278:3).

For Butler, however, chivalric punctillio and Puritan casuistry were merely symptoms of a far more pervasive human tendency — of "that primal energy," as Alvin Kernan defines it, "which drives the world toward the strange grotesque shapes it assumes" in all satire.[14] Kernan reminds us that great satire conceives of folly and vice in positive rather than in negative terms — more as an active presence or force than as absence or loss of value. "The better authors of satire," to Kernan, "have been literary Manichees who have shown an ancient and powerful force operating constantly and expressing its own nature through all lands and times."[15] "Dullness," that great, weighty, and dark source of all uncreative and destructive energy in Pope's *Dunciad*, admirably illustrates the idea; for Pope's word is "broad enough to cover the wide range of idiocy and viciousness portrayed in all satire."[16]

Butler also employs the word "dullness" in Pope's sense of a laborious activity or drudgery, but more frequently his name for this potential is "ignorance." Like dullness, ignorance is a precipitous and increasing force or weight. For ignorance, as described in the *character* of an "Ignorant Man," has "the same operation with the wiser part of the world as lead has in the test of metals, that being apply'd to gold carries away all the baser metals that are mixt with it . . ." (p. 282). As a source of energy, it is, like Zeal or enthusiasm, a dehumanizing power that turns its possessor into a mere machine; and Butler's "Fanatic," an early sketch of Swift's "Mechanical operation of the spirit," is a "Puppet Saint, that moves he knows not how, and his Ignorance is the dull leaden Weight that puts all his Parts in Motion" (p. 128).

Though conventionally the word "ignorance" implies an absence (and of course it is caused by the want of knowledge — particularly self-knowledge), Butler's ignorant are distinguished by their efforts to disguise and overcompensate for their shortcomings; for Butler, then, intense energy, dislocated from intelligence, is the primary characteristic of ignorance. As he observed in his notebook, under the heading "Learning and Knowledge," nature "relieves the Necessities of those, who are ashamed to have them known to others" by "perswading them they injoy that which of all things they are the most destitute of: And hence it come's that no men are so indefatigable Drudges in all manner of Sciences, as those to whom Nature has allow'd the weakest abilities to attaine to any perfection in them: for Duncan are commonly observ'd to be the hardest Students, as those always prove the most passionate Lovers, that meet with the most Coy and disdainfull Mistresses" (p. 289).

In business, the energies of ignorance emerge in the bureaucratic passion for red tape; in society, they appear as a preoccupation with clothes and manners; in education, as an academic interest in form and method rather than in substance; and in government, as a concern for the letter rather than for the spirit of the law. Wherever stupidity, ineptness, and moral flaccidity use words, acts, or attentions to make the simple and plain difficult and obscure, the trivial seem significant, the low seem high — there, Butler suggests, we are confronted with ignorance.

Hudibras is a satire of ignorance in this sense of the word. Butler's hero is introduced to us both as a "domestick" knight (a justice of the peace) and as a knight "errant": he is "Great on the Bench, Great in the Saddle" (I, i, 23). In the Knight's first words in the poem, spoken to his squire as they set out upon adventure, Hudibras says:

> We that are wisely mounted higher
> Then Constables, in Curule wit,
> When on Tribunal bench we sit,
> Like Speculators, should forsee,
> From *Pharos* of Authority,

Portended Mischiefs farther then
Low Proletarian Tithing-men. (I, i, 708 - 14)

The saddle, a surrogate of the tribunal bench, is, like the "oratorial machines" in Swift's *Tale of a Tub,* a means of achieving altitude, of being seen; in *Hudibras,* it is also a means of seeing "farther" — of magnifying "Portended Mischiefs." This tendency to make much of little — to turn a bear-baiting into a Jesuit plot against Puritan solidarity, or a skimmington into a pagan rite — is the means by which Hudibras' ignorance justifies itself. The knight's fondness for words is another example of this tendency, for language is the primary means by which men invest insignificance with importance. "Some occult design doth ly/In bloudy *Cynarctomachy,*" the knight at one point informs his squire, and "sure some mischief will come of it:/Unless . . . we averruncate it" (I, i, 745 - 46; 750 - 52). And Butler comments in a note to these lines that "Cynarctomachy signifies nothing in the World, but a Fight between *Dogs* and *Bears,* though both the Learned and Ignorant agree, that in such words very great Knowledge is contained: and our Knight as one, or both of those, was of the same opinion." Butler adds, in explanation of "averruncate": "Another of the same kind, which though it appear ever so Learned, and Profound, means nothing else but the weeding of Corn."

In religious matters, the energy of ignorance appears as an exquisite sensitivity (a "strict tendernes") to the slightest doctrinal difference or offense. Butler observed in his notebook that "zeal is no use without Opposition and Conscience has no way to show its Tendernesse, but in seeking Occasion to take offence at some thing or other, and the more slight and triviall the better, for its strict tendernes, and Innocence appears to be the greater, and the world will not be apt to suspect the Fayth and integrity of those, that are severe and scrupulous in small matters" (301:3). Thus, in men of a spiritual or intellectual calling (in men like Sir Hudibras), ignorance is a conjuring as well as a magnifying power, creating a specious existence for the qualities it lacks. Assuming, as it does, that great energy in external actions implies a great motivating spirit, and that energy always seems great when it is expended upon small matters, the ignorant mind concludes that the greatest concern with the smallest matters betokens the largest spirit. For this reason, Hudibras tends to internalize and spiritualize the trivial matters of sense that concern him, to turn them into questions of honor or conscience, and then to magnify them in words and actions. Believing that "th'Immortal Intellect/ . . ./Is free from outward bruise or maim,/Which nought external can expose/To gross material bangs or blows" (II, i, 191 - 96), his responses are intended as gestures of contempt for material security and physical safety.

But, of course, Hudibras cannot ignore sense: his bruises ache, his stomach growls, and his nose is assaulted by the fecal smells of his own fear. His spiritual pretensions are vain illusions: his paunch and rump are his only real burdens:

> . . . as *Aeneas* bore his Sire
> Upon his shoulders through the fire:
> Our Knight did bear no less a Pack
> Of his own Buttocks on his back:
> Which now had almost got the upper-
> Hand of his Head, for want of Crupper.
> To poise this equally, he bore
> A *Paunch* of the same bulk before:
> Which still he had a speciall care
> To keep well cramm'd with thrifty fare;
> As White-pot, Butter-mild, and Curds. (I, i, 287 - 97)

In the end, Hudibras' preoccupation with reason, honor, love, and conscience merely convinces us of his soullessness, his crass materialism, and his gross corporeality. The "inner man," a phrase which is used frequently in the poem for "soul" or "Conscience," is in his case the stomach; moral *sound-ness* (Butler puns on the word) is a vocal mannerism, the "sound and *twang of Nose*" (I, iii, 1157 - 58); and conscience is a garment whose "*Wear-and-tear*" may be "patch'd-up, and turn'd" (III, i, 1182 - 83). And what we have been saying of Hudibras' moral and intellectual energies applies as well to his physical energies: these too are compensatory, expended in this case in the name of a heroic spirit the knight does not possess. In general, Hudibras' efforts in this direction are failures, comic accidents, or necessities imposed by circumstance, as when we read that it was always the case with Hudibras, "in all his feats of Arms, when least/He dreamt of it, to prosper best" (I, iii, 531 - 32).

This comic conception of the self-betraying and self-defeating tendency of ignorance underlies the form of *Hudibras*, the nature of which, according to Richmond P. Bond, is "so complex in its origin and purpose and method that it defies final classification."[17] Bond is speaking of the classification of Butler's poem as a species of bur-

lesque, the general class to which he nevertheless provisionally assigns it under the name "Hudibrastic," a species of "low burlesque"
which places subject above style, and degrades a general (as travesty
degrades a particular) literary model through an undignified
treatment.[18] (Bond contrasts the Hudibrastic and the travesty with
the "high burlesque" mock-poem and parody, forms which place
style above subject, and borrow respectively a general and particular
literary manner to convey an unworthy subject.) But Bond is also the
first to admit that his tidy paradigm of burlesque forms provides in-
adequate space for Butler's poem. Though *Hudibras* treats a subject
of some degree of seriousness, and though its manner is obviously
coarse, its hero is not, for one thing, sufficiently elevated to permit
that stylistic denigration which characterizes low burlesque. Moreover, the process of degrading the hero is not caused solely by
rhetorical contrast, as is normally the case in high burlesque. Bond
concludes that Hudibras is "neither a trivial nor a dignified personage" as he is given to the reader, and that Butler both
"caricatures" the knight "and also places him in an heroic
framework." As a result, Bond finds the procedure of the poem "antithetical and dangerous"; its technique, "confusing."[19]

Bond is not alone in remarking about the complex nature of the
poem. James Sutherland has observed that "*Hudibras* contains
burlesque elements, but is not itself a burlesque poem";[20] and John
Wilders assigns to it the antithetical functions of both the mock-
heroic and the Hudibrastic. At times, he says, its literary allusions
"emphasize the meanness of the characters in comparison with their
epic trappings. . . . But the antithesis between form and subject also
acts in the opposite direction, the presence of coarse characters and
'low' actions within a heroic framework reflecting critically upon the
literary conventions themselves."[21] Edward Ames Richards urges us
to ignore Bond's related species of parody, travesty, mock-heroic,
and Hudibrastic as a "confusing field of esthetic relativities."
Richards suggests, instead, that we regard *Hudibras* as a "burlesque" in the simplest sense of that term — as "variation or distor-
tion."[22] And Ruth Nevo, who sees the poem at "the heart and center
of the [burlesque] mode in its historical seventeenth century sense,"
nevertheless observes that a contemporary like Dryden exempted
Butler from his general condemnation of the form.[23] Clearly, Bond
did not exaggerate in observing that "the greatest obstacle to consistent nomenclature [in this area] has been the nature of Butler's
poem."[24]

Notwithstanding the formal uniqueness of *Hudibras*, the obstacle that Bond speaks of is in large part, I believe, created by our expecting Butler's poem to conform to a preconceived pattern of burlesque — *either* to the treating of a dignified subject in an undignified manner *or* to the belittling of an undignified subject by means of dignified treatment. We expect Butler's method to be one or the other — low burlesque or high burlesque — but not both. The opening lines of Dryden's *Mac Flecknoe* — an example of the high burlesque (mock-heroic) procedure — provide a standpoint from which to appreciate the formal peculiarities of *Hudibras:*

> All human things are subject to decay,
> And when Fate summons, monarchs must obey.
> This Flecknoe found . . .

Here, the meanness of Flecknoe is intensified because the formality and the generality of the language in which he is considered is appropriate to the consideration of a true monarch. Ian Jack quotes these lines to illustrate his notion that "the characteristic mode of satire in *Hudibras* is the opposite of the mock-heroic" — not a form of burlesque at all; it is simple "low satire." Butler's method, he argues, "is that of straightforward 'diminution' "; his subject is "as different as possible from that of the romantic epic poet . . . and his style is equally remote from that of heroic verse. . . . The essence of low satire could not be more simple."[25] Jack is commenting in these words upon the opening lines of *Hudibras* (those beginning: "When civil fury first grew high/And men *fell out* they knew not why"); and we might well agree that, in this particular passage, Butler's method is "simple."

But is it true of the poem generally? We might also agree that the simplicity of the opening lines consists in an undignified treatment of the subject, religion, if by "treatment" we mean Butler's use of rough doggerel, coarse diction, and comic rhyme. But how shall we regard the heroic or romantic framework of the poem, its archaism and learned allusions which are clearly elements of a dignified nature? Or are such matters properly thought of as belonging to the subject rather than the "treatment" of the poem? Often, this "over-simple" distinction between subject and style is difficult to make in passages of *Hudibras*. The following lines — conveniently localizing something akin to burlesque incongruity in a simile — may serve to illustrate Butler's general procedure in the poem:

> The Learned Write, *An Insect Breeze*,
> Is but a Mungrel Prince of *Bees*,
> That Falls, before a Storm, on Cows,
> And stings the Founders of his House;
> From whose Corrupted Flesh, that Breed
> Of Vermine, did at first proceed:
> So ere the Storm of war broke out
> Religion spawn'd a various Rout,
> Of Petulant Capricious Sects,
> The Maggots of Corrupted Texts,
> That first Run all Religion down. (III, ii, 1 - 11)

From one point of view, we have the elements of simple mock-heroic here. Religion, the *tenor* of the figure, is clearly conceived of as a low subject: the "Petulant Capricious Sects" have been "spawn'd"; they are the "Maggots" of corrupted texts. Then too, the vehicle of the figure, what we shall call the "treatment" of the subject, is deliberately made "learned" or dignified: the Sects are compared to a *Prince* of Bees which has *proceeded* from cattle, the *Founders of his House*. Butler's treatment does not, however, belittle the subject as does the solemn commonplace with which Dryden begins *Mac Flecknoe*. Quite the contrary: whereas Dryden's lines point up the *difference* between the decay of monarchs and the decay of Flecknoe; Butler's force upon us the *similarity* between the generation of insects from "Corrupted Flesh" and the generation of religions from "Corrupted Texts." Flecknoe's pretensions to dignity define a set of values that mock him; he appears insignificant because his clothes are too large for him. In *Hudibras*, the values claimed by the hero are themselves mocked; and they indict the hero only insofar as they are themselves made to appear shabby. Hudibras' clothes suit him perfectly; they are out-of-date and threadbare.

Butler's method here and, I think, generally in the poem is anything but *simple*. Combining the functions of burlesque and low satire, he sets forth incongruities (between the ideal and the real, the high and the low) only to reduce both elements to a common level of absurdity. We might consider this method to be that of an anti-poet, of one who has lost faith in the ethical norms of his age and in the moral efficacy of traditional poetic means. Butler's skepticism extends to the very conventions of poetry which, like the conventions of learning and heroism (the scholastic hair-splitting and legal wrangling of the knight and squire, the invocation to the muse of Withers and Prynne, and the mock-catalogue of bear-baiters), stand as mere empty forms in *Hudibras.*

Butler's doggerel measure is an even more pervasive illustration of this attitude. "People expect a 'marked rhythm' to imply something worth marking," Walter Bagehot observed; "they are displeased at the visible waste of a powerful instrument. . . . The burst of metre . . . incident to high imagination, should not be wasted on petty matters which prose does as well. . . ."[26] Hudibrastic octosyllabics deliberately violate this law for comic effect — metrically inciting an expectation of significance that is subsequently unsatisfied. The metricality of the line is designed to exploit the phonetic value of words at the expense of their semantic value. As we are told at the beginning of Part II, "those that write in *Rhime,* still make/The one *Verse,* for the others sake" (ll. 27 - 28). The insistence of Butler's doggerel meter and doggerel rhyme acts as a powerful determiner; it is capable of synthesizing, truncating, and fracturing words, irrespective of their meanings:

> And Pulpit, Drum Ecclesiastick,
> Was beat with fist, instead of a stick;
> > (I, i, 11 - 12)

> There was an ancient sage *Philosopher,*
> That had read *Alexander Ross* over;
> > (I, ii, 1 - 2)

> Us'd him so like a base *Rascallion,*
> That old *Pyg-* (what d'y' call him?) malion . . .
> > (I, iii, 327 - 28)

Verse that can thus reduce language to mere sound provides the perfect vehicle for the expression of a system of debased values. A similar speciousness exists in many of the metaphors in the poem. Ruth Nevo has termed these "burlesque similitudes," their principle residing in "a concertina-like expansion and contraction of dimensions." There may, she says, "be a disparity between the quantitative treatment and the triviality of the thing treated; or between the magnitude of the simile's vehicle and the littleness of its tenor; or vice versa. . . ."[27] But, as we noted in the lines comparing religious sects and vermin, Butler's figures are only formally metaphorical —

they are more properly described by what will later be defined as "false wit." And we might note here that, although Addison himself appreciated that Butler was ridiculing false wit in lines like those just quoted, he objected to the public's fondness for Hudibrastic wit for its own sake.[28]

What we respond to in such structures is, finally, not incongruity, but congruity that is false because purely formal. If Butler's figures are "burlesque" in any sense, it is that they surrender the function of true wit (the making of truth intelligible, as Butler defined it) in order to become self-destructive puns; resemblances and congruities of sounds or syllables — not ideas — are wittily used to reveal their own falseness. In effect, they function precisely as Butler's hero does and, I believe, as do the heroic and learned elements in the larger structure of the poem.

Perhaps, then, the closest we can come to defining the nature of *Hudibras* is in the complex terms of Pope's description of bathos: the deliberate vulgarizing of content so as to "depress what is High," *together with* a style that manages to "raise what is Base and Low to a ridiculous Visibility." "When both these can be done at once," Pope explained, "then is the *Bathos* in Perfection; as when a Man is set with his Head downward, and his Breech upright, his Degrida-tion is compleat: one End of him is as high as ever, only that End is the Wrong one."[29] Alvin Kernan has observed that Pope was touching here on one of the chief problems of the satirist, the dif-ficulty of showing "that the mad world he constructs is truly mad, that it is the breech which is up, not the head."[30] In *Hudibras*, however, the distinction between high and low, the head and breech ends of things, is deliberately blurred. As Hudibras comments (in lines that could have been the inspiration of Pope's), "*Beards*, the nearer that they tend/To th'*Earth*, still grow more reverend:/And *Cannons* shoot the higher pitches,/The lower we let down their breeches" (II, i, 261 - 64). Most satire points out man's moral failure to live up to his professed ideals, but Butler's indicates the unreality of these ideals and the folly or villainy of those who appear to prac-tice them. "Dishonor, tho a Negative, is Real," he observed in some verse fragments in the "Poetical Thesarus"; "But Honor [is] Nothing but a Jugler['s] Spell . . . That aime's at no Designe, but to exempt/The Mean, and Despicable, from Contempt."[31] Our highest moral claims are, therefore, just so many "Intrigues and Projects" which "Compass by the Properst shows,/What ever [our] Designes propose";[32] and the more scrupulous we are about such matters, the more energy we expend in their pursuit, the more we stand convicted, Butler felt, of our own folly or fraud.

III *Plot*

Although Butler's rejection of the standards by which satire normally judges human behavior creates special problems for the critic attempting to define the formal nature of *Hudibras*, readers have encountered little difficulty in understanding the general satiric intention of the poem. Just as Butler's irreverent attitude toward the conventions of poetry and romance is unmistakably conveyed in the very materials of the poem, so there can be no uncertainty that Sir Hudibras is given to us as an ignorant fool — as a character who indicts himself by his own actions. Thus, by means of the plot of the poem we are made aware of the nature of ignorance.

Though the "story" with which Butler began provided the general outline of only the first part of *Hudibras*, the central idea of Part II and its third part sequel may be seen as a natural outgrowth of the poet's original creative impulse. That impulse, as we have already suggested, was the exposure of the falseness of the heroic view of life — a pattern of lies and pretenses that was formally embodied in romance and actively practiced, Butler believed, by the Puritans. Parts I and II of *Hudibras* — the ultimate victory of the fiddler over the knight, and the knight's unsuccessful suit of a widow — comprise, then, the conventional matter of romance: "for what else/Is in [romance]," Butler observed, "but *Love* and *Battels*"? (I, ii, 5 - 6). Accordingly, the narrative unity of all three parts of the poem is "heroic" — or some more or less consistent treatment of heroic materials.

Part I, "th' Adventure of the *Bear* and *Fiddle*," is the story of the knight's victory and defeat at the hands of a group of bear-baiters. The "heroic" action of the episode is taken up with two battles: one in the second canto in which Hudibras and Ralph manage (largely by accident) to stop a bear-baiting by dispersing its promoters and spectators and by arresting and confining in the stocks its central figure, a fiddler named Crowdero; the other in the third canto in which Hudibras and Ralph are defeated and confined in the stocks — the first of a series of reversals of romance conventions. The transition between these two battles is also conveyed in two scenes: the first of these (iii, 25 - 292) describes the routed bear-baiters as they regroup for a concerted attack upon the knight and his squire; the second (iii, 297 - 412) depicts the lucky warrior as an unlucky lover. Hudibras is a rejected suitor who — having "resolv'd . . . either to renounce [his lady] quite,/Or for a while play least in sight" (ll. 366 - 68) — nevertheless believes that his premature victory in canto ii "might work upon her" (ll. 378):

> So from his Couch the *Knight* did start,
> To seize upon the Widow's heart;
> Crying with hasty tone and hoarse,
> *Ralpho*, dispatch, To horse, to horse. (iii, 409 - 12)

The accidental encounter which follows is of course pure farce — the collision of the panting lover and the angry bear-baiters — but this confrontation also seems designed to challenge the orthodox critical assumption that love is a suitable subject in heroic literature. Butler calls attention to this implicit criticism at the beginning of Part II where, after announcing that he will "observe *Romantique* Method" by exchanging "rusty Steel" with "Love's more gentle stile" (1 - 5), he pretends to defend his poem in an ironic note to these lines: "The beginning of this Second Part may perhaps seem strange and abrupt to those who do not know, that it was written of purpose, in imitation of *Virgil*, who begins the IV Book of his *Aeneides* in the very same manner. . . . And this is enough to satisfy the curiosity of those who believe that Invention and Fancy ought to be measur'd (like Cases in Law) by Precedents, or else they are in the power of the Critique" (p. 100).

The reference in Part I to the knight's love for the widow is not, then, a hastily contrived link between the two parts of the poem; instead, his love is an important element of its "*Romantique* Method." Butler must fairly soon have recognized the limits of his initial ridicule of chivalric military exploits — the physical, external absurdities of the knight-errant. But love — or the pretense of love — reveals the internal workings of his hero, the complex casuistry and knavery which were Butler's chief interests in the study of human behavior. The more damaging moral exposure of the knight in Part II represents, then, not a change in the poet's conception of his hero;[33] it is an extension of his original satiric purpose to a different dimension of the hero's character. Moreover, Hudibras' interest in the widow becomes the crucial motive of subsequent action in the poem. It impels the hero toward his defeat in the second battle and his subsequent humiliation in the stocks, and it spurs his efforts in Part II to regain his former standing as a knight.

This development of the action begins with the widow's arrival at the place of the knight's confinement, a reversal of the traditional romantic rescue of a lady by a knight. Indeed, Hudibras' suffering is reduced to the unheroic "labor" of an expectant mother awaiting delivery:

> She vow'd she would go see the sight,
> And visit the distressed *Knight*,
> To do the office of a Neighbour,
> And be a *Gossip* at his Labour:
> And from his wooden Jayl the Stocks
> To set at large his Fetter-locks,
> And by Exchange, Parole, or Ransome,
> To free him from th'Inchanted Mansion. (i, 87 - 94)

In one other respect, Hudibras' lady departs from her prototype. The disdain of conventional mistresses for their lovers is, in the widow's case, an outright contempt for Hudibras that is formalized in her perverse taste of loving "none but onely such/As scorn'd and hated her as much" (I, iii, 335 - 36); and the unlikely tasks that she assigns the knight are contrived only to reveal his folly and dishonesty. Thus, in Part II (i, 825 ff.), the widow offers Hudibras the opportunity of immediate freedom and future matrimony if he will undergo a whipping, a bargain he readily accepts but does not honor. Instead, he additionally blackens his character by attempting to make Ralph his proxy for the whipping (ii, 441 ff.), a compromise that the squire threatens to resist with force. The ensuing quarrel is interrupted by the appearance of a skimmington — a folk ceremony practiced against shrewish wives — which the hypocritical Hudibras interprets as a heathen custom that is disrespectful to "that *Sex* . . . To whom the *Saints* [Puritans] are so beholding" (ii, 773 - 74). His harangue to the procession is countered by a barrage of rotten eggs and of an even more odoriferous substance that turns the knight and squire "in quest of nearest *Ponds*" (l. 886). On the strength of his bold attempt to assert feminine honor, Hudibras resolves to swear that he has undergone the whipping enjoined by the widow; yet, after his most recent humiliation, even his self-confidence is shaken, and, fearing "what *danger* might accrue,/If she should find he *swore* untrue" (iii, 47 - 48), he seeks the astrologer Sidrophel to learn "how farr the *Dest'nies* take my part" (l. 96).

In a sense, then, the widow becomes the satirist's accomplice by controlling the actions of the hero and by determining the topics of self-defeating discussion. In the first canto of Part II, the narrator speaks in only 219 lines; the remaining 705 are dialogue, over half of which (366 lines) are given to the widow. In the still more dramatic first canto of Part III, she again has the largest part (477 lines); and, even more significant, she is allowed the final say in the poem in "The Ladies Answer to the Knight." Quite literally, she takes over from the author the job of exposing romantic pretensions; and she assumes at times a mask of naiveté, as when she first refuses to rescue Hudibras from the stocks —

> . . . for a *Lady* no ways *Errant*
> To free a *Knight*, we have no warrant
> In any Authentical *Romance*,
> Or *Classique Author* yet of *France*:
> And I'de be loath to have you break
> An Ancient *Custom* for a freak,
> Or *Innovation* introduce
> In place of things of *antique* use. (i, 785 - 92)

But the widow more often voices Butler's own point of view, as in the following criticism of Hudibras' use of romantic poetry in courtship:

> Hold, hold, Quoth she, no more of this,
> Sir *Knight*, you take your aim amiss;
> For you will find it a hard *Chapter*,
> To catch me with *Poetique Rapture*,
> In which your *Mastery* of *Art*
> Doth shew it self, and not your *Heart*:
> Nor will you raise in mine *combustion*,
> By dint of high *Heroique* fustion:
> Shee that with *Poetry* is won,
> Is but a *Desk* to write upon. (i, 583 - 92)

In general, we might note, women do not fare well in Butler. In the notebook, they are spoken of with almost Medieval animosity as the latter-day Eves who introduce their men to the lies and cheats of proselitizing priests. In *Hudibras*, Butler makes a point of saying that Puritan women were the easy tools of Parliament in its appeals for money and plate to maintain the army. Actually, Butler is no more sympathetic in his treatment of the widow and of the two other women in the poem. Together, they not only expose the unreality of the idealized woman of romance, but also embody the standard

targets of traditional antifeminist satire. Hudibras' lady is cynical
and cruel; the wife who appears with her hen-pecked husband in the
skimmington is a domineering shrew; and the character of the "bold
Virago," Trulla, is implicit in her name. The fact that the women
appear to fare better than the men in the poem, or that Butler has
permitted each of them to contribute to the ridicule of Hudibras, is
testimony of his awareness not of feminine virtue but of masculine
ignorance.

Part II concludes with another ironic comment on conventional
heroism. At the end of the third canto, we see Hudibras spurring his
"lofty Beast" from "Danger, Fears, and Foes" and thereby beating
"at least three lengths, the wind" (ll. 1186 - 90). Earlier in this canto
(ll. 543 ff.), Hudibras quarrels with the astrologer, Sidrophel; accuses
him of trafficking with the devil and of the theft of his identity and
purse (an allusion to the spurious second part of *Hudibras);* and
sends Ralph to "fetch us/A *Cunstable* to seize the Wretches" (ll.
1015 - 16). But, while the knight holds Sidrophel and his assistant at
bay, the astrologer feigns death; and Hudibras regards it "now, no
longer safe,/To tarry the return of *Raph*" (ll. 1149 - 50). Instead, he
will make Ralph "by force abide,/What he by gentle means deny'd"
(ll. 1179 - 80) — that is, he will stand as the knight's proxy in the
whipping. "For if [Ralph] scape with *Whipping* now," Hudibras
reasons, " 'Tis more than he can hope to do./And that will disengage
my *Conscience*, Of th'*Obligation*" (ll. 1175 - 78). Thus, Hudibras
wins a sort of victory — momentary, to be sure, and won by deception and treachery — but this sort of victory, Butler suggests, is what
we find in heroic literature.

The third part of *Hudibras* has never been much admired, one
criticism being that (notwithstanding Butler's designation of it as the
"last part") it is inconclusive. The narrative of the poem is first interrupted in the second canto by two overly long summaries of recent history, and then it is virtually ignored for the two "heroic
epistles" ("Hudibras to his Lady," and "The Ladies Answer") at the
end of the poem. The historical accounts — one (ll. 495 - 998) given
by a Presbyterian (identified in the "Key to Hudibras" as the
Leveller, John Lilburne); the other (ll. 1011 - 1498) by an Independent (more certainly Anthony Ashley Cooper, Earl of Shaftesbury)
— point up the "Carnal Interests" of the two dominant factions in
the Puritan party; and, more generally, these accounts suggest what
happens to all revolutionary movements when what "us'd to urge
the Brethren on" is at last "divided, shar'd, and gone" (ll. 37 - 38).

Bishop Burnet may have had these two passages in mind when he recommended Butler to the Princess Sophia as "the truest historian of the affairs of England from the death of Cromwell to King Charles his Restoration."[34] Then too the satiric approach to the heroic view of life is more direct and explicit in Part III than in the two preceding parts of the poem. Relying less on the oblique method of rhetorical contrast and dramatic irony, Butler now requires his hero to reveal the true motives behind his "heroic" actions. When Ralph discovers that Hudibras plans to "leave him in the *Lurch*," he goes directly to the widow, and, in hopes of marrying her himself, informs her of the knight's deceit (i, 125 - 48). To punish Hudibras, who next attends the lady himself, the widow first tells him that he is sought by the ghost of Sidrophel, and then stages an "*Anti-masquerade*" of "*Furies, and Hobgoblins*" to frighten the knight into confessing not only that he ventured "*to betray,/And filch the Ladies Heart away*" (ll. 1175 - 76) in order to gain control of her money, but that he is a liar, a hypocrite, a breaker of vows, and a more perfect devil than the supposed spirit that is interrogating him.

This humiliation of the knight has been taken by some readers as the real conclusion of the poem. W. O. S. Sutherland, for one, says that "the finality lies in the character of Hudibras rather than in the accumulation of incident. The heroic point of view has been degraded and discredited. There remains nothing new for Hudibras to do. The poet has made his point."[35] As we have seen, however, it is unlikely that Butler would have felt that the folly and the ignorance of mankind are ever concluded. Indeed, there is much that is new for Hudibras to try. His experience through the poem does not cause him to repudiate the falseness of his values but to recognize the danger in risking life and limb to attain them. Since honor is nothing more than a word, man cannot afford to employ more than words to attain it. This method, Ralph persuades the knight, is the real heroic way — in fact as well as in fiction:

> So all their Combats now, as then,
> Are manag'd chiefly by the Pen.
> That does the Feat, with braver vigours,
> *In words at length, as well as Figures.* (iii, 419 - 22)

Henceforth, Hudibras will fight only verbal battles — in the courts of law and in heroic epistles. Butler's final indictment of heroic literature marks only the end of his hero's career as a knight-errant; but it constitutes a new phase in his career as "domestick" knight.

Butler's third part conclusion to the antiheroic action of *Hudibras* also serves to draw the theme of Puritan-Independent rivalry into the total imaginative structure of the poem, reducing the apparent differences between Presbyterian and Independent, fool and knave, to a common ground. Throughout the first two parts of the poem, these differences are increasingly underscored; and they result, at the beginning of Part III, in the mutual renunciation of Hudibras and Ralph, a separation that is underscored by the contrasting historical accounts of the Puritan movement in canto ii. But at the most dramatic point in this development — the moment at which the knight openly confesses the base motives of his "holiness" — the action strangely reverses itself. Butler contrives this effect with considerable care by abruptly ending the burlesque *Walpurgisnacht* of the beginning of canto i in order to leave Hudibras "in the dark alone," unable to sleep for his aching bones, yet "still expecting worse, and more" (l. 1329). Then, a voice "in a feeble Tone," like the small voice of his weak conscience, speaks "these trembling words":

> . . . Unhappy Wretch,
> What hast thou gotten by this Fetch?
> Or all thy tricks in this New Trade,
> The Holy Brother-hood o'th' Blade?
> By Santring still on some Adventure,
> And Growing to thy Horse a Centaure?
>
> . . . .
>
> Night is the Sabbath of Mankind
> To rest the Body and the Mind.
> Which now thou art deny'd to keep,
> And cure thy labour'd Corps with Sleep.
>
>   (i, 1339 - 52 — the original in italics)

This voice, which continues in fits, summarizes Hudibras' "late Disasters" from the engagement with the dogs and bears to his most recent dispute with Sidrophel. So "impudently" does it "own/What I have suffer'd for and done" (ll. 1381 - 82), Hudibras confesses, that it can only belong to one of the earlier fiends who is trying now to "steal me . . . from myself" (l. 1380).

As the reader discovers, however, this alter ego of the knight is only Ralph, who, in "vent'ring to betray,/Hast met with Vengeance the same way" (ll. 1383 - 84); and, believing himself to be alone, he has been lamenting his own condition. Butler does more than merely confuse the two characters here. Knowing that Hudibras is "*too obstinate,/To be, by me prevayl'd upon*," that "*the Devil . . . only can prevail upon ye*" (iii, 154 - 55; 159 - 60), Ralph is willing to damn himself (i.e., accept the role of devil) in order to damn the knight. Hudibras, on the other hand, is willing to accept his consignment to a place among the devils as long as it is made by an Independent whose devilish identity is admitted; for he says to this devil:

> 'Tis true, Quoth He [Hudibras], that intercourse
> Has past between your Friends and ours,
> That as you trust us in our way,
> To raise your Members and to lay:
> We send you others of our own,
>
> . . . .
>
> Have us'd all means to propagate
> Your mighty interests of State,
> Laid out our Spiritual Gifts, to further
> Your great designs of Rage and Murther.
> For if the Saints are Nam'd from Blood,
> We onl' have made that Title good,
> And if it were but in our Power,
> We should not scruple to do more.
> And not be half a Soul behind,
> Of all Dissenters of Mankind. (i, 1529 - 46)

Revealed in his true nature, neither speaker is obliged to maintain a role or to defend an opinion; and, for the first time in the poem, Hudibras and his squire achieve a sort of harmony.

CHAPTER 4

The Argument and Imagery of Hudibras

THE general drift of *Hudibras* criticism is historical; it has attempted, in general, to fix the poem more securely in the social, political, and ecclesiastical contexts of Butler's era rather than try to make it more available to our own. To a large extent, the serious students of *Hudibras* have been source hunters — like the author of the early "Key" to the identities of Butler's characters — or, more recently, they have been interpreters of historical allegory. Its editors have been either antiquarians — like Zachary Grey in the eighteenth century — or historians — like John Wilders in the twentieth.[1]

This historical emphasis is of course justified by the topical nature of Butler's satire; but *Hudibras* warrants at least one other critical approach — one which has the added merit of recommending the poem to modern readers. Butler's notebook provides a clue to such a reading; for, viewed in the light of the ethical and philosophical reflections recorded in it by the author, *Hudibras* displays a pronounced interest in general human nature.[2] Such a view of the poem reveals that Butler's satiric attention is most frequently directed to man's ethical pretensions — specifically upon the faculty which, improperly used, encourages mankind in general to place his own kind above all others and a particular man to place himself above all others of his own kind. As we have seen, that faculty for Butler was reason, the natural mark of human preeminence itself, but the source as well of all man's artificial distinctions, such as his absurd pretensions to an inhuman sainthood and to a heroism that presumes to justify such a claim. Sir Hudibras, the man of reason, Puritan knight extraordinary, is thus the embodiment of these tendencies — a sort of burlesque Everyman. *Hudibras*, as we shall see, is a satire on mankind, a redefinition of the sine qua non of man as folly and viciousness.

I *Beasts and Men: Folly and Ignorance*

In describing *Hudibras* as a satire on man, I am placing the poem in a specific category of satire. This type of satire embraces such varied examples as the Earl of Rochester's *Satyr Against Mankind* and the fourth book of Swift's *Gulliver's Travels*, and it characterizes itself by attacking not particular individuals or groups — deviations from an assumed hierarchy of normative values — but the human species as a whole.[3] Necessarily concerned with essential human nature, such satire typically finds the conduct of men less consistent than that of animals with the norms of nature. George Boas has assigned the term "theriophily" to this point of view, and has traced its source for French literature to Montaigne's *Apology for Raimond Sebond;* to Plutarch's *Moralia;* and to the literary paradox, the brief, playful essay that contradicts prevailing opinions on human nature.[4] References in Butler's writings to all three of these sources suggest his awareness of the theriophilist tradition.

Near the beginning of *Hudibras*, for example, Butler refers to a pertinent passage in Montaigne's *Apology* in which the author, "playing with his Cat,/Complaines she thought him but an Ass" (I, i, 38 - 39).[5] In the second canto of Part II of the poem, he specifically cites Montaigne as a dealer in paradox — as one who makes "*true* and *false, unjust* and *just,*/Of no use but to be discust" (ll. 9 - 14). Then too, Butler's notebook concludes with a collection of "Contradictions" which are only a trifle less playfully intended than the paradoxes that provided the context of the French essayist's theriophily. We read here, for example, that "Beasts that have no Apprehension of Death th[at] wee can perceive, live more according to Nature, and some Brutes are better qualifyd with those things that wee call virtues in our selves then men who professe the Greatest Mortifications . . ." (422:1); that "the Breed of Mankind is Naturally less able to help it selfe as soon as they are produc'd into the world, then those of any other Creatures" (423:1); and that "Bees and Ants seem to manage their affayrs with little less reason of State, and more Justice then men: being wholy free from those Distractions which the vices of Avarice Pride and Ambition produce in Governments" (443:2). And, in Butler's manuscript commonplace book, he concludes a statement on the disorder which "Speculative Truths" would create in world affairs with an observation that might have come from a twentieth century ethologist: "beasts of ye same Species that have no notion of Truth at all, live quieter among themselves then men who for y^c most part are not much better furnish'd; & yet have more then they know how to make good use of."[6] Though Butler's scorn of the Royal Society's experiments on animal life is expressed in a work like the mock-scientific paper "on Dr. Charlton's Feeling a Dog's Pulse," the notes just quoted reveal, nevertheless, the keen interest in animals that was generated by the new scientific empiricism of the age. Such observations, it is worth pointing out, are quite different from those found in Pliny's *Natural History*, which is a repository of fanciful animal lore that turns up again and again in works like John Lyly's *Euphues*, Robert Burton's *Anatomy of Melancholy*, and, anachronistically, Pope's *Essay on Man*. Such lore, by revealing the "correspondences" between the rational and irrational links on the great chain of being, emphasizes the principle of hierarchical degree in nature. But scientific investigation was changing all this by bringing man and beast much more closely together, and Butler's moral interpretation of this data reflects this change — whether he wished to or not.

Butler himself probably did not believe that animals possess reason, but then we have already observed that his view of reason made this absence no great disadvantage. Given to man not at the Creation, as traditionally assumed, but at the Fall, Butler believed that reason was punitive as well as redemptive — for, as we have noted, man was then "forc'd to drudge for that Food and Cloathing which other creatures receive freely from the Bounty of Nature" (363:3), and he was also sentenced to discover truth by his own efforts (288:1). But just as clothing — the peculiarly human sign of both guilt and weakness — had, in Butler's view, come to be "his greatest Indulgence" (457:1), the means of concealing human frailty, so reason — a second mark of man's fallen condition — had become the agent of his pride, the means of concealing or disguising truth when it was not to his advantage. Reason, if used as God intended it to be — in conjunction with the senses, as the means of discovering order in nature and of ascertaining man's proper place within that order — was to be a safeguard against a recurrence of the Fall. However, as men use it, reason is both the chief weapon of knavery and the primary target at which knavery aims. For Butler, then, reason is more often a curse than a blessing, as it is more often than not used unnaturally. "'Tis not true reason I despise but yours," Rochester wrote in his *Satyr;* "I think Reason righted but for *Man*." Butler would have concurred with this view, and such views would have led him to question the supposed inferiority of irrational animals.

We must somewhat indirectly approach Butler's theriophily by way of a passage included under the rubric "Reason" in his notebook. "Men without Reason are much worse than Beasts," he says, "because they want the end of their Creation, and fall short of that which give's them their Being, which Beasts do not, but are Reliev'd for that Defect, by another way of Instinct, which is nothing but a Kinde of Implicit Reason, that without understanding why, directs them, to do, or forbeare those thinges that are agreeable, or hurtfull [to] their Particular Natures: while a Fool is but Half Man, and Half beast, is depriv'd of the Advantages of both, and has the Benefit of Neither" (339:3). To understand fully the relationship of this remark to Butler's view of human nature, we must first recognize the broad or generic sense which the word "fool" bears in this passage. The word is used in the same way in Butler's comprehensive prose *character* of a "Fool." There we notice again the same two outstanding characteristics of the type — his relationship to an animal and his mechanical behavior. Wanting reason, men lack the capability of self-direction — "that which give's them their Being" — and are manipulated by others or by their own ungoverned passions. Butler's *character* of the fool first describes the type as "the skin of a man stuff'd with straw, like an alligator, that has nothing of humanity but the outside." Then, in a passage which anticipates Locke's distinction between animals and machines (the "motion" of animals "coming from within"; that of the machines, "from without"), Butler says that the fool "is not actuated by any inward principle of his own, like an animal; but by something without him, like an engine; for he is nothing of himself, but as he is wound up, and set a going by others" (p. 275).

Under the rubric "Wit and Folly" in the notebook, Butler more specifically identifies folly with "Natural Madnes," a congenital deprivation of reason in man; and he contrasts it with rational nature that has in two ways been corrupted — first, with what we must call "accidental madness" ("that which men fall into by Accident or their own ungovern'd Passions"); and, second, with what he himself calls "Artificiall Folly" or "Industrious Ignorance" (327:2). In this section of the notebook, men without reason (natural madmen or "fools" in the specific sense) are not placed below the animals but, to their advantage, are on a par with them. Butler observes, for example, that the "Providence that Cloaths and Feede's Beasts, because they know not how to help themselves, Provides for all Sorts of Fooles, that are aequally incapable of Relieving themselves without it" (329:1). And again, under the same heading, he observes that the "Craft and Subtlety which she [Nature] has given to all helpless Creatures (as Hares, and Foxes)," she has granted as a compensation for the absence of reason in natural madmen; "and hence it is that Fooles are Commonly so fortunate in the world, and wiser men so unhappy and miserable" (326:2).

On the other hand, men whose reason has been corrupted ("accidental madmen" and the ignorant) are, throughout Butler's work, associated, to their disadvantage, with animals. The prose *characters* are filled with illustrations. The "Imitator," for example, is said to have "a Kind of Monkey and Baboon Wit, that takes after some Man's Way" (p. 136); the "Rude Man" is "the best Instance of the Truth of *Pythagoras's* Doctrine, for his Soul past through all Sorts of brute Beasts before it came to him, and still retains something of the Nature of every one" (p. 195); the "Henpect Man" is "a Kind of preposterous Animal, that being curbed in goes with his Tail forwards" (p. 81). Proselytes are "Cattle driven by the Priests of one Religion out of the Quarters of another" (p. 130); a "Rabble" is "the greatest and most savage Beast in the whole World" (p. 197); an "Inconstant" man is like a deer (p. 243); a "Pedant," like a cock (p. 188). The "Court-Beggar" is a dog (p. 72); the "Bumpkin," a horse (p. 75); the "Antiquary," a moth (p. 27); the "Proud Man," an owl (p. 77); the "Fantastic" a cormorant (p. 95) — and so on through Butler's one hundred ninety-odd *characters*.

In addition to these animal analogies of corrupted rational nature (some of which, to be sure, may be no more than instances of conventional invective), we also find a number of images of a certainly more philosophical source — those that refer to the new science of mechanics. As we have already noticed, Butler's *character* of a "Fool" regards mechanical behavior as one of the characteristics of the man without reason; but we now learn that it is also a characteristic of those who misuse reason since, in so doing, such men reject the human responsibility of self-direction (the act "which give's them their Being") and allow themselves to be governed by others or by their own passions. Descartes, we should note here, opposed the theriophilist position by arguing that animals lacked a soul and were only mechanically activated. In the *Discourse on Method*, he writes that, "if there were machines with the organs and appearance of a monky, or some other irrational animal, we should have no means of telling that they were not altogether of the same nature as those animals" (V, 56). Butler, however, employs the Cartesian argument against reason in animals to criticize man's improper use of reason.[7] The *character* of the "Formal Man," for example, begins with the analogy of "a Piece of Clockwork, that moves only as it is wound up and set, and not like a voluntary Agent" (p. 237); and this type of figure again appears in the *characters* of the "Affected Man" (p. 193) and of the "Hypocrite" (p. 218). The "Fanatic," we will recall, is described as "a Puppet Saint, that moves he knows not how, and his Ignorance is the dull leaden Weight that puts all his Parts in Motion" (p. 128). In other *characters,* mechanical imagery is used to describe the effect of an action upon its irrational object. Thus the "Fidler" is "like the spring of a clockwork-motion, that sets all the puppets a dancing, till 'tis run down" (p. 274); the "Musitian" "winds up souls, like watches" (p. 293); and, since the "Knave" or Deceiver is himself a misuser of reason, he is said to be "very skilful in all the Mechanics of Cheat" (p. 214). Hudibras even thinks of his own "wit" as "a gin" (I, iii, 391); for this reason, Ralph speaks of the "mechanick Pawes" of the Puritan clergy (iii, 1245); and, in Part II, the wizard Sidrophel's feigning death in battle is likened to the fox's trick of eluding pursuers, an act which comes "not out of Cunning, but a *Train*/Of *Atoms* justling in his Brain" (iii, 1121 - 22).

As the result of these passages, we recognize that Butler's relegation of "fools" to a place beneath that of the animals applies more to men with reason who use that faculty unnaturally or improperly than to "men without Reason" — applies more to accidental madmen and to the ignorant than to natural madmen. In the "Satire upon the Imperfection and Abuse of Human Learning," for example, Butler touches upon the peculiar vulnerability of man by noting the unfortunate effect of custom on reason:

> For Custom, though but usher of the school,
> Where Nature breeds the body and the soul,
> Usurps a greater pow'r and interest
> O'er man, the heir of Reason, than brute beast;
> That by two different instincts is led,
> Born to the one, and to the other bred;
> And trains him up with rudiments more false
> Than Nature does her stupid animals (ll. 9 - 16, *P.W.)*

According to Boas, "the theoretical — if not the psychological basis of Theriophily is that the beasts . . . are more 'natural' than man, and *hence* man's superior."[8] Animals and idiots, of course, have little ability to be anything but natural; and when, for whatever reason, they become more like human beings — as in the case of monkeys and baboons — Butler believed that they are "worse and more deformd then those Creatures that are all Beast" (280:2). Reason, on the other hand, confers upon its possessors both a new nature and a new freedom to achieve it. When men with reason — either consciously or unconsciously — violate this nature, they become knaves or fools (in the comprehensive sense of the word) and "much worse than Beasts." Butler did not, then, categorically deny the value of reason, he vigorously attacked anti-intellectualism and philosophical scepticism by calling either one "the Modern False doctrine of the Court" (286:3). Nevertheless, the misuse of reason seemed to him inevitable — and the world a place given over to knavery and folly.

The specific type of "folly" or deviation from human nature which is our chief concern in a reading of *Hudibras* is ignorance, the irrational behavior caused, as we have noticed, not by the want or impairment of reason (as in natural or accidental madness), but by the want of knowledge or the empirical data with which Butler believed reason properly worked. (Pope arrived at a similar notion at the beginning of Epistle II of *An Essay on Man*, describing man's paradoxical nature as one that is "Alike in ignorance, his reason such,/Whether he thinks too little, or too much.") Since ignorance frequently uses reason to disguise these wants, Butler conceived of it as a positive rather than a negative condition, calling it, as we have seen, "*Artificial* Madness" or "*Industrious* Ignorance." In his customary imagery, reason in the ignorant man is a tailor that clothes both the mind and the world, thereby concealing human deficiencies and refashioning nature according to human desires. Just this sort of intellectual effort, Butler believed, produced the tradition of humane learning with which his hero was *internally* "accouter'd," as the poem so significantly puts it (I, i, 235 - 36). We are informed that Hudibras *wore* his wit only on holidays "as men their best Apparel do" (I, i, 50), and that his linguistic habits are "a particolour'd dress"; " 'Twas *English* cut on *Greek* and *Latin*,/Like Fustian heretofore on Sattin" (I, i, 97 - 98). Butler regarded the "Instrumentall Arts" of grammar, rhetoric, and logic as "Fopperys" (412:3) that were used to "make senseless and impertinent Reflections upon things, and having fitted them with as insignificant

Tearmes, they passe for learning" (407:3). Of Aristotle, whose works
for the knight are what books of chivalry were for Don Quixote,
Butler observed that "his chiefest care had been to make his
Systemes of her [nature] rather Artificiall than true, and to agree
among themselves very prettily, but perhaps without any great
regard to Truth or Nature" (403:4). Hudibras' mind, then — as it is
presented in the verse "character" which opens the poem — is more
descriptive of an intellectual type (the scholastic "realist"), or an
ethical type (the "ignorant" man) than of the "true blew"
Presbyterian that he no less certainly represents.

In general, students of *Hudibras* have offered historical ex-
planations for the knight's scholasticism. John Wilders, for example,
comments that "Hudibras is typical of the early Presbyterians, many
of whom were university men. Ralpho resembles the unlettered independent sectarians of the mid-seventeenth century who laid claim
to divine inspiration."[9] But the contrasting mental equipment of the
knight and his squire also represents two extreme forms of ignorance, or unnatural human behavior: intellectualism and anti-
intellectualism. For Butler, as we have said, the *natural* use of reason
lies between these two extremes. True knowledge, he believed,
begins and ends with the senses. Through perception, the understanding receives images of the natural world; reason attempts to put
these confused images into their original order in nature; and sense,
again, is called upon to verify this mental order in the material world
(336:1). Thus ignorance is likened to a man who has replaced a lost
eye with one of glass, "which though it cannot see, can make a Show
as if it did, and is proof against al those accidents that use to destroy
true ones" (333:2). The use of the senses is conspicuously absent in
the thought of both Hudibras and Ralph; in the knight, it has been
replaced by the machinery of rationalism; in the squire, by imagination.

The knight's rationalism, his virtual blindness to the material
world, and his total commitment to the abstract intellect are the keys
to our reading of *Hudibras* as a satire on man. The importance of this
character trait might best be represented by comparing the folly of
the English knight with that of his Spanish prototype, Don Quixote.
Both are victims of illusion — the product of learning ("industrious
ignorance") in the former, and, as Butler noted, of humours (accidental madness [327:2]) in the latter. Quixote is so obsessed with
the idea of chivalry that he *sees* the images of romance in the real
world: windmills actually *look* to him like giants. But Hudibras sees

little or nothing in the world; he "forsees" (intellectually) a subversive plot against Puritanism in an innocent bear-baiting. Logic is the mode of his folly or ignorance, and the assumption that man is *animal rationale* is the illusion on which his logic customarily works. Indeed, the very form of Butler's poem — and especially the first part of it[10] — is determined by Hudibras' mind. Part I begins and ends with a formal argument between the knight and his squire about the rational nature of man. Between these two sections (or against this background), Hudibras' battle with the bear-baiters is told. Thus the logical demonstration of human rationality provides an ironic context for the dramatic revelation of human nature.

II   *The Argument of* Hudibras, *Part I*

Hudibras' argument with Ralph in canto i develops from the knight's attempt to justify prohibiting a bear-baiting. In part, his reasons are understandable, if not justifiable: for bear-baiting was regarded as a dangerous and ungodly pastime; and, as a Puritan magistrate, Hudibras regarded it as his duty to maintain public safety (ll. 721 - 32) and to uphold Christian piety (ll. 789 - 94). Another and, in the knight's mind, more important reason for stopping the bear-baiting is his quixotic interpretation of the sport as a Jesuit plot to divide the Puritan party (ll. 733 - 52). His reasoning to substantiate this delusion might be described as an argument that proves the natural aggressiveness of men. Hudibras argues as follows: it is not in the nature of animals, as it is in men, to fight among themselves (ll. 753 - 78); but men may teach animals to fight among themselves (ll. 779 - 88); therefore, if a dog and a bear are about to fight, men must have taught them.

Hudibras' first proposition assumes that animals lack reason and the ability to "discourse," for earlier in his speech (and generally throughout the poem), verbal disputation is equated with physical fighting ("where the first does hap to be,/The last does *coincidere*" [ll. 719 - 20]); and the first part of his demonstration of the exclusively human nature of fighting consists of the rallying cries and shibboleths of Parliamentary polemic ("Frail *Priviledge, Fundamental Laws . . . thorough Reformation . . . Covenant . . . Protestation,*" etc. [ll. 755 - 64]). His second proposition assumes that, although animals lack reason, they are endowed with a sort of "wit" which enables them to "know" and to "learn" but not to conceive of a second "interest" for which men customarily fight — God. This notion would have accorded with Butler's personal view of the dependence of faith upon reason; for, as he observed in his notebook, "no Irrational Creature is capable of it [faith]: and if we will not allow this, we must of necessity acknowledg that it depend upon ignorance, which is worse, for no man can believe anything but because he do's not know it" (338:1). Men have made gods of Beasts, Hudibras argues; "but no Beast ever was so slight,/For man, as for his God, to fight:/They [animals] have more wit, alas! and know/Themselves and us better then so" (ll. 775 - 78). What the animals "know" that prevents their worshipping men as gods can only be their own nature and that of man — and that is as much as saying that they know that men are not their superiors.

Hudibras' argument in Part I is, to say the least, inconsistent: it begins with the assumption that men are superior to animals, and concludes that they are not. But ridicule of the knight's faulty logic is only a part of the satiric function of this episode and of the long quarrel about Presbyterian authoritarianism that Ralph makes of it. More important than this is the fact that the argument throws a new light upon the traditional notions of the value of reason and the nature of man. Now it is important to recognize that Hudibras' argument is itself purely rational; it is neither founded upon nor verified by sensory data. It is an example, therefore, of that unnatural use of reason that Butler called "Artificial Madness" or "Industrious Ignorance." Nevertheless, two truths (for Butler at least) ironically emerge from Hudibras' remarks. The first is dramatically demonstrated in the second canto: reason — used for disputation — is the cause of strife among men; the rational prowess by which the knight *foresees* and hopes to avert mischief actually promotes it. The second truth, a corollary of the first, is that men are more brutal than animals.

Homo est animal rationale is the traditional definition of man found in text books of logic since Aristotle, and this axiom is customarily opposed to an example of *animal irrationale*, traditionally the horse. This logical commonplace provides the point of departure for Butler's examination of man, and is therefore clearly marked in the poem. To one as "profoundly skill'd in Analytick" (I, i, 66) as Hudibras, this statement was as familiar as his own name. When Ralph, in his personal attack upon Presbyterianism, charges that no difference exists between synods and bear-baitings, the knight promptly counters by saying that "both are *Animalia* . . . but not *Rationalia*":

> For though they do agree in kind,
> Specifick difference we find,
> And can no more make *Bears* of these,
> Then prove *my horse is Socrates.* (I, iii, 1277 - 82)

Or again, in the courtship scene of Part II, when the knight's lady wittily assails his virility by likening him to a *"Roan-Guelding,"* Hudibras with perfect seriousness replies: "I am no *Horse* . . . I can argue, and discourse" (II, i, 721 - 22). In defense of an anthropocentric world, Descartes argued that man is unique; as an understanding sign-user, he is an inimitable creation; a beast, on the other hand — even the most sophisticated one — may be mechanically fabricated. Butler pushes this notion to its logical extreme: if reason makes men autonomous, the absence of it makes animals mere clockwork machines. Thus the bear-baiting episode begins with an implicit recognition of the uniqueness of human reason; as the knight and his squire ride out, we read that "they now begun/To spur their living Engines on":

> For as whipp'd Tops and bandy'd Balls,
> The learned hold, are Animals:
> So Horses they affirm to be
> Mere Engines, made by Geometry,
> And were invented first from Engins. (I, ii, 53 - 59)

But the clarity of these distinctions between a rational order capable of ethical choice and a bestial order that is not rational is only sporadic in the poem; rather, throughout Part I, Butler seems intent upon blurring such distinctions. We notice, for example, the ironic effect of Hudibras' attempt to differentiate between Synod-men and bears:

> A *Bear's* a savage Beast, of all
> Most ugly and unnatural,
> Whelpt without form, until the Dam
> Have lickt him into shape and frame:
> But all thy *light* can ne're evict
> That ever *Synod-man* was *lickt;*
> Or brought to any other fashion
> Then his own will and inclination. (I, iii, 1305 - 12)

Hudibras' beard — at various times the mark of his philosophical status, his religious commitment, and his virility — is generally a symbol in the poem of the knight's manhood: tails symbolize bestiality. Yet we notice how the widow manages to parry Hudibras' proposal of marriage: since "*Tayls*," she insists, "by Nature sure were meant/As well as *Beards*, for ornament," she will "never marry *man* that wants one" (II, i, 743 - 48). To which Hudibras replies: "If she [nature] ever gave that *boon*/To man, I'l prove that I have one;/I mean by *postulate Illation* . . ." (II, i, 761 - 63) — that is, if necessary, he will use his reason to prove that he is an animal.

Then, in the following references to the use of language and reason (distinctively human abilities), Butler wittily confuses the orders of man and beast. Hudibras is said to speak Greek "as naturally as Pigs squeek" (l. 52); Latin was for him "no more difficile,/Then to a Blackbird 'tis to whistle" (ll. 53 - 54); and his linguistic fluency is described as a "gabble" (l. 101). Like Mahomet, the knight was "linkt" by "fast instinct/Of wit and temper" to the ass and pigeon (ll. 230 - 32). Ralph too "understood the speech of Birds/As well as they themselves do words" (ll. 541 - 42), a gift which Butler attached generally to hermetic philosophers.[11] Hudibras' highly vaunted skill in "Analytick" further confuses the species:

> He'd undertake to prove by force
> Of Argument, a Man's no Horse.
> He'd prove a Buzzard is no Fowl,
> And that a *Lord* may be an Owl;
> A Calf an *Alderman*, a Goose a *Justice*,
> And Rooks *Committee-men* and *Trustees*. (ll. 72 - 76)

In short, argument and disputation, the "*Arms* that spring from [human] *Skulls*," place men in the class of horned beasts (ii, 439 - 40).

It is possible, of course, to interpret the last of these passages as merely a part of the mock-heroic machinery of the poem. However, insofar as heroism is a peculiarly human attribute, the heroic assumed an ethical as well as a literary significance for Butler. Even Hudibras, in one of his more candid moments, admits "there's but the twinckling of a *Star*/Between a Man of *Peace* and *War*" (II, iii, 956 - 57). In the opening description of Hudibras, the knight is formally presented to us as a man living a double life: he is "amphibious" in that his knightly duties are both domestic and errant, "either for Chartel or for Warrant:/Great on the Bench, Great in the Saddle,/ . . . styl'd of *War* as well as *Peace*" (ll. 21 - 28).

But these professional alternatives are then translated into ethical and, finally, into zoological terms; and distinction becomes all but impossible:

> But here our Authors make a doubt,
> Whether he were more wise, or stout.
> Some hold the one, and some the other:
> But howsoe're they make a pother,
> The difference was so small, his Brain
> Outweigh'd his Rage but half a grain:
>
> . . . .
>
> As *Mountaigne,* playing with his Cat,
> Complaines she thought him but an Ass,
> Much more she would Sir *Hudibras.* (ll. 29 - 40)

And, if heroism makes men resemble brutes, it makes animals seem more human. Bruin the bear is actually ennobled by his actions in the battle. Checked on all sides by the knight and his squire, by the dogs, and by the fleeing rabble, the bear "valiantly" takes his stand, "leaving no Art untry'd, nor Trick/Of Warrior stout and Politick"; he resolves that, "rather than yield,/To die with honour in the field":

> But one against a multitude,
> Is more then mortal can make good.
>
> . . . .
>
> While manfully himself he bore,
> And setting his right-foot before,
> He rais'd himself, to shew how tall
> His Person was, above them all. (iii, 37 - 84)

"Armed" (ii, 259) and "clad in a Mantle *della Guer"* (ii, 253), Bruin is led "to the lists" (ii, 152); he is "a bold Chieftain" (iii, 41), a "Champion" (iii, 143), a "Warrior" (ii, 152), an Achilles (iii, 139 - 46). The human bear-baiters, on the other hand, are mere "Auxiliary men,/That came to aid their Bretheren" (ii, 67 - 68).

III *Animal Imagery in* Hudibras

The frequency with which animals and men are rhetorically and poetically associated in *Hudibras* is perhaps the most telling evidence of Butler's interest in the indistinctness of human and animal nature. Animals furnish by far the largest number of images in the poem, and every human figure in Part I is characterized by some sort of animal reference. Many of these terms are, of course, colloquial forms of abuse that are commonplace in comedy. Hudibras is called an ass or an "old Cur," and he chases the bear-baiters as a cat does mice (iii, 463 - 64); Puritans are stubborn as mules (II, ii, 229), and are hated worse than "dogs and snakes" (i, 742). But many are fresher than these conventional terms of abuse, or they function in quite other ways. Hudibras' "amphibious" nature, for example, makes him a rat, equally at home on land or water (i, 27); at one point in the battle, Orsin "ferrets" him out for single combat (iii, 236); the knight grasps his gun with a hand that resembles the talons of a goose contracting in death (iii, 525 - 28); and he seizes upon his lady's heart as an owl seizes upon a mouse (iii, 403 - 10). Talgol, the butcher-turned-bear-baiter, addresses Hudibras as "Vermine wretched,/As e're in Meazel'd Pork was hatched;/Thou Tail of Worship, that dost grow/On Rump of Justice, as of Cow" (ii, 687 - 90).

The sectarian Ralph is also described as a "*Mungrel*" bred by the Puritan church (II, ii, 554 - 55); as a "Wild-foul" (i, 507); and, because of his ability to understand only dark matters, as an owl (i, 552). The bear-baiters are regarded collectively as "tame Cattel" (iii, 253), and are said to be infected with some "*Oestrum*" (an insect which attacks cattle [ii, 495]). Crowdero, the fiddler, strings his bow with a hair from his beard rather than from a horse's tail (ii, 125 - 28); he is called a "whelp of Sin" (ii, 956); and he is addressed as "thy Curship" (ii, 959). Orsin, the bear-warden, was nursed by a bear, and bred in Paris Garden (ii, 168 - 72). The fierce Talgol is characterized by his trade, the butchering of animals (ii, 298 - 326); Magnano is "fierce as forrest-Bore" (ii, 335); and Trulla, the "bold Virago," is stout as a female bear, the only species, according to philosophers, in which the female is not the weaker sex (ii, 381 - 82). Cerdon's disputatiousness makes him a ram or bull (ii, 438); and Colon's identity has all but merged with that of his horse, except that the former "was much the rougher part,/And alwayes had a harder heart" (ii, 451 - 52).

Perhaps it is only natural that rural bear-baiters are described in animal terms, but the animal imagery of *Hudibras* has a broader application than this appellation suggests. We are told, for example, that Orsin conducts the baiting as a lawyer antagonizes the defen-dant and the plaintiff in a legal action, an analogy elaborated in

much the way that Ralph later argues that Presbyterian synods are
bear-baitings:

> So Lawyers, lest the *Bear* defendant,
> And Plaintiff *Dog*, should make an end on't,
> Do stave and tail with *Writs of Error*,
> *Reverse of Judgement*, and *Demurrer*,
> To let them breath awhile, and then
> Cry whoop, and set them on agen. (ii, 161 - 66)

In a note explaining the words "staving" and "tayling" as "terms of
Art usd in the *Bear-Garden*," Butler ironically adds that "they are
us'd Metaphorically in several other Professions, for moderating, as
Law, Divinity, Hectoring, etc."[12] Elsewhere, we find that an
astrologer is a "Vulture" (II, iii, 27); a Puritan, a "Dog distract, or
Monky sick" (i, 209 - 10). Puritans make converts in the way that
men catch birds, fish (II, iii, 7 - 14), or elephants — i.e., with the use
of a female as bait (ii, 585 - 88). Men in love are like animals; love
draws them by the tails (II, i, 431 - 32; II, iii, 67 - 72), and rides them
as horses (II, i, 890; II, iii, 559 - 60). A lover is "tawed [tanned] as
gentle as a Glove" (II, i, 880), and is, of course, given horns by an
unfaithful mistress (II, ii, 711 - 12). A wife is a "clog," or manacle
used on beasts (II, i, 654). Cupid's arrow wounds Hudibras in the
"*Purtenance*" (the "inwards" of an animal [iii, 318]). His lady is a
"Mule that flings and kicks" (iii, 331 - 32), and she must be taken as
a bird is caught (II, i, 278), or as a "tumbler" (a dog) catches a coney
(iii, 353 - 55). Human teeth and nails are "fangs" and "claws" (i,
743); skin is "hide" (ii, 708); a nose, a "snout" (iii, 357); a beard, a
"mane" (II, i, 750). Men in general are "Moral Cattle" (II, ii, 200).

If it be objected that we are taking these animal analogies too
literally, that what is here offered as a satirical consideration of the
relationship between man and beast is nothing more than conventional raillery, let us notice some examples of the reverse situation —
descriptions of animals in human terms. These are less numerous
than the former for the simple reason that there are fewer animals
than men in the poem; nevertheless, such descriptions occur with
sufficient frequency to suggest a satiric pattern in which men are
brutalized and animals humanized. We might, in this connection,
notice the rhetorical preeminence bestowed upon Hudibras' horse in
the "Argument" to canto i: Hudibras' "*Arms and Equipage are
shown;/His Horse's Vertues, and his own.*" (This is the horse, by the
way, that stirred no more at spur or switch "then *Spaniard* whipt" [i,

423 - 24].) Butler's animals engage in disputes (i, 716), and are subject to the influence of the stars (i, 605 - 606); indeed, their indifference to wealth is the only distinction (except that of religion,
noted earlier) that is insisted upon in the poem (II, i, 469 - 70).
Talgol, the butcher, is said to have "sent so vast a Colony [of
beasts] /To both the underworlds" (ii, 319 - 20) that he made "many
a Widow . . . and many Fatherless" (ii, 303 - 304). A similar
domesticating of beasts occurs in Hudibras' opening argument
against bear-baiting: Is it not enough, he asks rhetorically there, that
we Purι*ans have risked "our Liberties, our Lives,/The Lawes,
Religion, and our Wives . . . For *Cov'nant* and the *Cause's* sake"?
And yet, he continues, in a bear-baiting, "*Dogs* and *Bears*,/As well
as we, must venture theirs" (i, 727 - 32). In their protection of the
dog and bear, Talgol and Orsin each strive to "deserve the
Crown/Of a sav'd Citizen," that ancient Roman recognition of service to a fellow citizen in time of war (ii, 287 - 92). We might also
note here that, while Orsin had grown up among bears, Bruin
"'mong the *Cossacks* had been bred" (ii, 267).

But perhaps the most convincing evidence that Butler consciously
used language to exploit the ambiguous natures of man and beast is
found in the classical allusions and in the bits of esoteric learning
that occur in the poem. To a remarkable degree, these appear to bear
upon just such an intention. For example, Romulus, the wolf-nursed
hero, is cited as the prototype of the bear-warden, Orsin (ii, 167 -
68); Crowdero is compared to the centaur Chiron (ii, 125 - 32). From
the analogy of the Persian legend of a horse that proclaimed a king,
Butler invents a Staffordshire festival "where Bulls do chuse the
Boldest King/And Ruler, o're the men of string" (ii, 133 - 38). From
the collection of Leblanc's *Travels*, he extracts and, in a note,
ironically defends the improbability of a tall tale about a bear
that "spous'd" an Indian princess and "got on her a Race of
Worthyes/As stout as any upon earth is" (ii, 283 - 86). In the wooing
scene of Part II, Hudibras defends his equine virility with a
reference to Semiramis of Babylon, a queen who, Butler explains in a
note to the line, "is said to have receiv'd Horses into her embraces"
(i, 713 - 15); like Pasiphae's, her taste for animal lovers was a punishment for her indifference to men (i, 387 - 98). In Part I, learned an-
tiquaries are cited to testify that man is the youngest of the creatures
— "For Beasts, when man was but a piece/Of earth himself, did th'
earth possess" (ii, 467 - 73); and Hudibras' lady summons
"*Philosophers* of late" to establish that "Men have fewer legs by

Nature," amplifying her remarks with an account of a German
boy who was adopted by wolves, "and growing down t'a man, was
wont/With *Wolves* upon all four to hunt" (II, 725 - 32).

The combined effect of many of these images and allusions, as we
have been suggesting, is to provide a sort of naturalistic accompani-
ment to the battle between Hudibras and the bear-baiters. These
references encourage the reader, by the middle of the third canto of
Part I, to believe that men behave like animals and that reason —
such as that used earlier by Hudibras to prove the distinctiveness of
man — leads to quarrelsomeness and brutishness. That the knight
and his squire should at this point renew their earlier argument is a
further joke at the expense of human nature, for neither imagination
nor reason has yet led them to the truth that the bear has learned
through simple experience:

> that they [men]
> For whom h' had fought so many a fray,
> And serv'd with loss of bloud so long,
> Should offer such inhumane wrong. (ii, 893 - 96)

It may appear that Ralph — whose fanciful use of animal analogies
for men exceeds any thus far demonstrated — has also learned this
truth: at one point, he remarks that "*Bears* naturally are beasts of
Prey,/That live by rapine, so do they [synods]" (iii, 1123 - 24); that
"the difference is, The one fights with/The Tongue, the other with
the Teeth" (iii, 1107 - 08); and he is contemptuous of the knight's
rationalist approach to the world, calling it "A fort of Errour, to
ensconce/Absurdity and ignorance" (iii, 1349 - 50). But Ralph's
position is also a case of special pleading, directed not at men in
general, but only at Presbyterians: "*Saints* themselves are brought to
stake," he says, and "expos'd to *Scribes* and *Presbyters,*/Instead of
Mastive-dogs and *Curs;*/Then whom th' have less humanity,/For
these at souls of men will flie" (iii, 1111 - 16). Though it may appear
to voice Butler's own views, Ralph's argument rests upon neither experience nor reason but upon a supernatural "gift" of inspiration.
He regards the knight's rational prowess as

> An Art t'incumber *Gifts* and wit,
> And render both for nothing fit;
> Makes *light* unactive, dull and troubled,
> Like little David in *Saul's* doublet. (iii, 1343 - 46)

Ralph's indictment of rational man is, therefore, just as partial as Hudibras' defense of him; and the squire's view serves as a means of concealing the speaker's own inhumanity while it attributes bestiality to those whose opinions differ from his own. Ralph earns his place beside the knight in the stocks at the end of Part I.

This confinement of Hudibras and Ralph is Butler's final act of comic revenge against mankind. Incapable now of public mischief (the stocks were described earlier in the poem as a harness that renders the body sensitive to "Spur and Switch,/As if 'twere ridden Post by Witch" [ii, 1157 - 58]), rational man ironically condemns himself. Interpreting literally Ralph's identification of Presbyters with "*Bears* and *Dogs* and *Bearwards* too," Hudibras fails to see the truth of what he logically denies: that rational man is "a strange *Chimaera* of Beasts and Men,/Made up of pieces Heterogene,/Such as in Nature never met . . ." (iii, 1315 - 19). For the careful reader of Part I of *Hudibras*, however, no amount of ratiocination can make him appear otherwise.

IV   *Male Chauvinism in* Hudibras, *Parts II and III*

In Part I of *Hudibras*, then, Butler satirized mankind by elaborating upon the ambiguous relations between rational man and the irrational beast. But what of the remainder of the poem, the conclusion of which took fifteen years to appear? Did the satirist relent in his attack upon general human nature as the memories of Commonwealth cruelty and hypocrisy receded? In parts II and III, Butler dropped the story of Hudibras' battle with the bear-baiters; and, as we have related, introduced the affair of the knight's wooing of a widow — moved, as he says, from the clash of "rusty Steel" in war to the "more gentle stile" of love. But, although a stronger relationship exists between parts II and III than between either of these sequels and Part I (or, to put it more precisely, although the narrative coherence of Part III is more dependent upon Part II than that of Part II is upon its predecessor), the general direction of the original satire remains unchanged in the latter parts. Human rationality — the chief cause of man's pride — is still the target. But the satirical stance is feminist rather than theriophilist; reason is judged now in relation to feminine common sense rather than to animal instinct. Butler assumes that his reader is at least aware of what might be called the male chauvinism of the seventeenth century — he expects us to identify human reason as masculine reason. Thus, as the satire

of Part I aims to elevate animals over men, that of parts II and III
aims to elevate women over men.

Traditionally, of course, woman occupied a place on the great
chain of being somewhat below man. True, a new note was beginning to be heard in some seventeenth century considerations of
marriage. In *Paradise Lost*, for example, Milton's Raphael asks:

> Among unequals what society
> Can sort, what harmony or true delight?
> Which must be mutual, in proportion due
> Giv'n and receiv'd. (VIII, 383 - 86)

And, along the same line, here is Hudibras' lady:

> . . . What does a *Match* imply
> But *likeness* and *equality?*
> I know you cannot think mee fit,
> To be the *Yoke-fellow* of your *Wit*. (II, i, 669 - 72)

But these speeches are special cases: Raphael's interest in equality in
marriage occurs in a discussion of the impropriety of human
"conversation" between man and beast, and Butler's lady is engaged
in parrying one of the knight's proposals of marriage. Milton
himself, who justified divorce on the grounds of an "unconversing
inability of *minde*" in *either* partner in marriage, nevertheless
reflects the male supremacist bias of his era by speaking of man as
"the perfeter sex." In *Paradise Lost*, Milton makes it abundantly
clear that order in the domestic state depends upon authority
residing in the hands of the physically and intellectually superior
husband. To deny the subordinate status of women, a spokesman for
the prevailing view wrote in 1635, "is to resist the Councell of the
Highest."[13] Yet this is precisely what Butler seems to be doing in
Hudibras; for he gives Trulla, the fierce virago - bear-baiter, greater
physical strength and courage than either Hudibras or her male
counterparts, and he makes the craft and common sense of the hero's
lady victorious over the masculine learning and intellect of her lover.

Butler took a special pleasure in turning a romance against itself in
this way; as we have already noticed, he regarded its effect (along
with that of the epic and panegyric) as anything but salutary, believing that its images of masculine virtue encouraged not emulation —
as apologists for the heroic optimistically argued — but moral
lassitude and complacency in its readers. On the other hand, the

humiliating images of men offered in satire and lampoon are morally efficacious. The latter are "more True" than the former, and are therefore "capable of doing Princes more good," he wrote in his notebook, "(for Panegyriques being nothing but Polite Flattery never did any)" (431:5). Thus, in serving to mask the real physical and spiritual weaknesses of men, the assumptions and conventions of heroic fiction supported the traditional belief in masculine superiority. And this belief was reenforced by another, that of the saintly but vulnerable female, fostered by romance. The appearance, in the second canto of Part II, of a skimmington — a social punishment performed "when o're the Breeches greedy *Women*/Fight, to extend their vast *Dominion*" (ll. 699 - 700)[14] — testifies to the persistence of these myths in the world of the poem. Hudibras errs in attacking the promoters of the skimmington, by mistaking their female victim — a shrew who belongs in popular antifeminist literature — for the idealized lady of courtly romance, or for her Commonwealth equivalent — one who "fixt" her man "constant to the *Party*,/With motives *powerful*, and *hearty*" (ll. 785 - 86). The persecutors are in fact his allies, for they are the enforcers of masculine supremacy in marriage.

Hudibras makes a similar mistake in his dealings with the widow. He assumes that this lady will respect the rules of romance, that she will exhibit the conventional submissiveness of her type in order to give him the opportunity to display his assumed superiority. But such an opportunity — the conventional testing of a knight — is pointless, and the lady knows it: she is after all an *experienced* widow. She assumes the role of the "lady" of romance — serving as the embodiment of Hudibras' desire and as the determiner of his words and actions — only to expose his weaknesses. Indeed, she is the satiric intelligence of the second and third parts of the poem. In Part I, Butler, the "satirist" or narrator, is himself the stage director, equipping his hero with "sufficient" reason, then retiring to the wings to watch him bring about his own undoing. But in the two following parts of the poem, Hudibras's mistress, the unnamed widow, is even more directly involved in the exposure of the knight. Endowed with wealth and with knowledge of the character of men, she becomes a baited trap for the knight when she obtains, at the opening of Part II, his release from the stocks at a price (true honor) that she knows he cannot pay, and thereby prompts him to a course of deception that she can expose whenever she pleases.

Quite understandably, Hudibras is the defender of the traditional

fictions about the sexes. Forced to surrender to the ignominy of the
stocks by one woman and then to purchase freedom at the equally
repugnant terms of another, the knight draws a final sanction of un-
justified self-esteem from the orthodox scale of being. Thus, the
argument of Hudibras' "Heroical Epistle" to the widow rests on the
premise that "Women first were made for Men,/Not Men for them"
(ll. 273 - 74). Milton, too, in the *Doctrine and Discipline of Divorce*,
maintained that "woman was created for man, and not man for
woman";[15] and, in *Tetrachordon*, he deduced from this premise a
peculiarly masculine grounds for divorce: "Seeing woman was pur-
posely made for man . . . it cannot stand before the breath of this
divine utterance, that man . . . joyning to himself for his intended
good and solace an inferiour sexe, should so becom her thrall, whose
wilfulness or inability to be a wife frustrates the occasionall end of
her creation, but that he may acquitt himself to freedom by his
naturall birthright, and that indeleble character of priority which
God crown'd him with."[16] And if masculine "priority" permits a
man to sever the bonds of matrimony, it can also, Hudibras reasons,
guarantee his right to tie them — even if the inferior woman in question is opposed to the idea. Reason can have it both ways. "It follows
then," the knight goes on,

> That Men have right to every one,
> And they no freedom of their own:
> [That] . . . Men have pow'r to chuse,
> But they no Charter to refuse:
>
> . . . .
>
> And that you ought to take that course,
> As we take you *for Bett'r or worse*
> And Gratefully submit to those,
> Who you, before another chose. (ll. 273 - 86)

These lines seem strangely direct language for the devious rhetori-
cian who never opened his mouth but "out there flew a Trope." But
Hudibras now realizes that the widow sees through his attempts at
fraud, and it is significant that this apology for masculine supremacy
is part of a longer apology for his own use of deception in courtship.
Casuistry and ratiocination, like the exercise of the masculine will,
are the "prerogatives" of rational men. He therefore locates the
cause of his present disgrace (the widow has both rejected his

proposal of marriage and exposed him as a liar) not in himself, but in the collapse of the established sexual hierarchy:

> . . . why should every Savage Beast
> Exceed his *Great Lord's Interest?*
> Have freer Pow'r, then he, in *Grace,*
> *And Nature,* o're the Creature has?
> Because the Laws, he since has made,
> Have cut off all the Pow'r he had,
> Retrench'd the absolute Dominion
> That Nature gave him, over Women. (ll. 287 - 94)

The prerogatives of *"Grace and Nature"* make men the lords of women as well as of animals. Masculine reason not only justifies its own faults; it makes feminine resistance to its arguments a violation of natural law.

But, while Hudibras and his brethren strive to maintain the prerogatives guaranteed them by tradition, the women in the poem make it quite clear that the traditional sexual hierarchy is no reflection of the relative capabilities of men and women. The bear-baiting Trulla wins Hudibras' sword and forces him to wear her petticoat; and Hudibras' lady, who senses the ironic possibilities in being able to rescue her knight from the stocks, attends him as a "gossip" assists at the "labour" of an expectant neighbor, but she hesitates to *deliver* him, however, because romance offers no precedent for such a demonstration of feminine ability.

Thus, as the imagery of Part I tended to brutalize men and humanize animals, that of parts II and III tends to feminize men and masculinize women. Intellectually, as well as physically, the women outclass the men in the poem — and they manage to do so even with the imperfect rational powers which their age assigned them. In "The Ladies Answer to the Knight," the satirical climax of the poem, the widow exposes the dishonesty of Hudibras' marital demands and of the concept of masculine "priority" which lies behind it. Hudibras' dishonesty is not a new discovery on her part but a demonstration that feminine intuition and experience are better at detecting fraud than masculine reason is at perpetrating it. Wealth is the real incentive of her "lover's" courtship, she says in a witty critique of amatory convention: "'Tis not those Orient Pearls our Teeth . . . But those we wear about our Necks,/Produce those Amorous Effects" (ll. 65 - 68); and, she continues, "these Love-tricks I've been vers't in so,/That all their sly *Intrigues,* I know" (ll.

73 - 74). But the widow is not shocked at the economic motives of marriage; she herself is a practical materialist:

> [Love,] where there's Substance, for it's Ground,
> Cannot but be more Firm, and Sound,
> Then that which has the slighter Basis,
> Of *Airey virtue, wit, and graces.* (ll. 105 - 08)

Hudibras' interest in her money "is Right," she concedes; it is "the Course,/You take to do't, by Fraud, or Force" (ll. 149 - 50) that arouses her indignation.

What prompts the widow to answer the knight at all is less her desire for personal victory over a man she has never taken seriously than her opportunity to strike at reason's self-begotten fiction of masculine power — a fiction that this representative man personifies in his every act and word. She would show all men that women cannot be tricked or coerced; that the power sanctioned by their rationally contrived myth of superiority is illusory — Hudibras, the man, testifies to its falsity; and that real power consists in the acceptance of often unflattering truths about human nature. Thus, the widow is quite willing to accept the role that men have given her sex — that of the passionate seductress of reason; in fact, she can even accept the biblical premise of this view, for she recognizes that the real power in a world of mortals is sexuality, not rationality:

> Though Women first were made for Men,
> Yet Men were made for them agen:
> For when *(out-witted by his Wife)*
> Man first turn'd Tenant, but, *for life,*
> If Women had not Interven'd,
> How soon had Mankind had an end?
>
> . . . .
>
> Then where's your Liberty of Choyce,
> And our unnatural No-voyce? (ll. 239 - 48)

It is not the rational disputation of men, she says, but "our more *Pow'rful Eloquence,*" that manages "things of Greatest weight,/In all the world's *Affairs of State*" (ll. 294 - 96).

We may be sure that Butler himself was not a feminist. Though his remarks on women in the notebooks are infrequent, most of those we find reflect the antifeminist prejudices of his age. Here, for example, is his observation about the psychology of women:

> The Soules of women are so small
> That Some believe th' have none at all;
> Or, if they have, Like Cripples, still
> Th' ave but one facu[l]ty, the Will;
> The other two are quite layd by
> To make up one great Tyranny:
> And though their Passions have most Powr,
> They are (like Turkes) but slaves the more
> To th' Abs'lute will, that with a breath
> Has Sovrain Powr of life and Death.
> And, as it's little Interests move,
> Can turne 'em all to Hate or love
> For nothing in a Moment turn
> To Frantique Love, Disdain, and Scorn,
> And make that Love degenerate
> T' as great extremity of Hate
> And Hate againe, and Scorn, and Piques
> To Flames, and Raptures, and Love-Tricks.[17]

At the same time, however, we must also notice that such remarks by Butler often appear in contradiction to one another — an indication perhaps of a weakening of prejudice, or of the strain involved in asserting it. Butler belittles women as the "weaker vessels," but he also appears to fear them for their sexual power (368:1), an inconsistency that reflects both the tradition that Satan chose Eve for his agent in Eden, and the current suspicion that priests use women as their chief means of proselytizing in families (319). Though Butler attempts to naturalize the salaciousness of women (as the motive of procreation [358:6]), he also observes that they differ in this respect from the lower creatures in whom it is the male, not the female, that is "allways ready to generate" (449:3). Of feminine morality, Butler said that the most to be expected of a woman can be expressed as only a "negative continence" (341:5): yet he also observed that chastity itself may become the source of feminine pride and the excuse for many other faults in the sex (341:6).

But, although Butler shared his age's estimate of feminine reason and virtue, he did not share its faith in the assumed intellectual and moral superiority conferred by masculine reason. We have already spoken of his attitude toward reason — that, though it is the means of surviving in a world of evil, it is also the root of human pride and villainy. The very faculty which can prevent the recurrence of Adam's original delusion had become through pride the means of man's subsequent self-delusion or ignorance. For this reason, Butler may at least satirically entertain the notion that the instinctive beast (326:2) or the lucky natural fool (who is guided by some sort of special providence [329:1]) is more than an equal match for rational man. And in *Hudibras*, we are suggesting, he makes a similar concession about the unreasonable, but cunning and wily, woman who is endowed with "Naturall Arts" of her own for turning men's heads (368:1). As for marriage, is that state of harmony guaranteed by the authority of a rational husband? Butler regarded marriage not as a state of order but as a condition of perpetual strife — as a conflict between the pride of masculine reason and the even stronger power of the feminine senses:

> Hence 'tis, they are no sooner made one Flesh,
> And both compounded int' a civil mesh;
> But Sexes next become the sole debate,
> And which has greater right to this, or that;
> Or whether 'tis Obedience, or Dominion
> That Man can claim a title to, or Woman,
> Untill the Issue has been fairly try'd,
> And legally found oftest for the bride,
> Who can reduce the most imperious Brave
> To be her Drudge, and Utensil, and Slave:
> To Husband takes the Idiot during life
> And makes him but a Helper to his wife.[18]

The moral and physical victories of the women in *Hudibras*, then, are a part of the strategy of Butler's satire against man — *animal rationale*. In his *Satyr Against Mankind*, Rochester said he would "be a *Dog*, a *Monkey*, or a *Bear*,/Or any thing but that vain *Animal*,/Who is so proud of being rational." In Part I of *Hudibras*, Butler used Rochester's dog and bear to ridicule man's pride in reason; in parts II and III, he takes up his "any thing," and makes it a woman, to achieve this end.

CHAPTER 5

Butler's Characters

ALTHOUGH none of Butler's prose *characters* was published in his lifetime, Robert Thyer, who first published 121 of them in *The Genuine Remains* (1759), surmised from the state of the author's manuscripts that some of these had been prepared for the press. In 1904, A. R. Waller republished these, together with sixty-six additional *characters* which Thyer had also transcribed from Butler's manuscripts. Subsequently, eleven more have come to light, eight of which had found their way into some numbers of the *London Magazine* (1825 - 26); one in the manuscript commonplace book (A "Schoolmaster"); and two (now referred to as "A Covetous Man" and "War") in Butler's holograph in the British Museum (included in Waller's reprinting of the notebook materials, but not as *characters* there[1]). This brings the total of Butler's *characters* to 198, not counting fragments.

According to Thyer, "most" of the *characters* he published had been dated by Butler; and they were "chiefly drawn up from 1667 to 1669."[2] Only two of these dates remain, however, that of the "Bankrupt" and of the "Horse-Courser" — 1667, October 6 and 8 respectively. By that date, the wave of Theophrastan *character* books — collections of prose sketches of social, psychological, moral, and professional types — had crested and subsided. In its place had come the historical *character*, a verbal portrait of an actual personage that was published singly or as an illustration within some larger context, and what Benjamin Boyce has named the "polemical" *character*, a vigorously biased description of a particular set of religious or political beliefs.[3]

Butler was no doubt familiar with the entire tradition of *character* writing (the Theophrastan Greek original was first translated into Latin by Isaac Casaubon in 1592), and we find traces of each of these varieties in his total output in the genre. With respect to subject, for

example, many of Butler's *characters* exhibit that English extension
of the moral portrait into the area of social types, a development
usually credited to the collection published under Sir Thomas Over-
bury's name, but including specimens attributed to John Webster,
Thomas Dekker, and others. There are in Butler's collection, of
course, a number of titles suggesting the older portrait of abstract
vices ("A Proud Man," "A Debauched Man," "The Luxurious," "A
Coward") that Joseph Hall popularized in 1608 in his *Characters of
Vertues and Vices,* the earliest English imitation of Theophrastus.
But in addition to the *character* of "An Hypocrite," Butler also gives
us "An Hypocritical Nonconformist" — the older moral interest existing here (and in "A Degenerate Noble," "A Huffing Courtier,"
and "A Corrupt Judge") as merely a modification of an existing
social type; moreover, it is clear that Butler regards the "Hypocrite"
not purely as a moral type (cf. Joseph Hall's more Theophrastan
counterpart), but as an ecclesiastical figure. This interest in social
analysis is shown even more clearly by the thoroughness with which
Butler surveys human occupations — the highest professions (legal,
religious, medical, and academic) and the lowest trades; and, within
these general categories, he makes even further distinctions, often
defining a professional hierarchy of complicity in an office: the legal
types, for example, rising from the lowly "Knight of the Post" and
"Justice of the Peace," through the "Pettifogger" and "Lawyer," to
the "Alderman" and "Judge" — and we might also find places here
for the peripheral figures of the "Catchpole," "Constable," "Jailor,"
and "Jurer."

The historical *character* — or, as David Nichol Smith suggests, the
deliberate blending of historical portrait and Theophrastan *character*[4] — is represented by Butler's "A Duke of Bucks" (Butler's pun-
ning allusion to George Villiers, Duke of Buckingham, a type of
perversion in human nature) and perhaps by "An Haranguer"
(William Prynne), "A Small Poet," and "An Hermetic Philosopher"
(Thomas Vaughn). Finally, in his portraits of ideological and
religious types (in "A Republican," "A Fifth-Monarchy-Man," and
"A Latitudinarian," for instance), and in his occasional extension of
characters to essay length ("A Modern Politician" runs to over seven
thousand five hundred words) we have examples of the late
polemical *character*. Butler's close relation to this tradition is also indicated by his borrowings from some of these earlier practitioners in
the form — particularly from specimens in John Earle's *Micro-
cosmography* (1628, 1633) and from the polemical pieces of Richard

Flecknoe and John Cleveland.[5] Butler's "Clown [or Rustic]," for example — one who "manures the Earth like a Dung-hill, but lets himself lye Fallow" (p. 131), — is clearly descended from Earle's "Plain Country Fellow," who "manures his ground wel, but lets himself lie fallow and untill'd." From Cleveland's "Character of a Diurnal-Maker" (1647), Butler drew such images as the "Curious Man's" "iron Chain . . . about the Neck of a Flea" and his "Iliads in a Nutshell" (p. 105), the "Fanatic's" "Portugese Horses" (p. 96), and the "Melancholy Man's" "falling Sickness" (pp. 97 - 98).

Of the emergence of the Overburian *character*, the development of which we have been suggesting in terms of Butler's production, W. J. Paylor observes that "The writer of the *Overburian Character* is not primarily interested in the texture of one particular fault out of which a man is neatly cut to the pattern of a dissembler or a flatterer. His criticism is centered upon the varied vices and mannerisms of the social types around him, and his portraits are influenced in their composition more by contemporary drama, satire and pamphlets, wherein these figures abound, than by classical Character."[6] The author of such *characters*, we might say, had become scientific in his approach to behavior — he is less interested in demonstrating the existence of universals in human nature than in recording the actual manners of certain classes of individuals. This change in view would have suited perfectly Butler's own empirical turn of mind. But there is an important difference between Butler's *characters* of social analysis (and his polemical *characters*) and those of his contemporaries and Overburian predecessors. Butler's method is reductive. Although he appears to be primarily interested in describing a multiplicity of types, what his *characters* in fact reveal is the persistence of one or two motives of folly or villainy inherent in almost every variety of human nature. Specifically these motivations are man's insatiable appetite for self-deception and his ingenuity in the use of human reason to devise the means of deceiving others. For all their apparent interest in contemporary manners, Butler's *characters* are firmly rooted in the moral assumptions of their author.

There is little value, then, in a statistical approach to Butler's *characters*. Butler himself comes close to suggesting this fact in the *character* of "A Cheat": "All the greater Sort of Cheats," he writes, "being allowed by Authority, have lost their Names (as *Judges*, when they are called to the Bench, are no more stiled *Lawyers*) and left the Title to the meaner only, and the unallowed" (p. 171). Butler is more interested in what he terms the "Callings" — the inherent

aptitudes or ruling passions — than in the "Professions" of his subjects. He is most interested, perhaps, in the discrepancy between
"calling" and "profession"; for this difference constitutes the satiric
situation of his *characters*.

The *character* of "The Cheat," for example, makes explicit the
close interdependence that Butler finds among his subjects: the
Cheat "is a Freeman of all Trades, and all Trades of his," it begins
(p. 170); and later: "He can do no Feats without the cooperating
Assistance of the Chowse [Gull], whose Credulity commonly meets
the Imposter half Way, otherwise nothing is done; for all the Craft is
not in the Catching (as the Proverb says) but the better half at least
in being catched" (p. 171). Often, two *characters* represent merely
two views of the same deception — as "A Popish Priest" and "A
Proselite," "A Lawyer" and "A Litigious Man," "A Mountebank"
and "A Medicine-Taker." "A Cully," or Dupe (a nonentity himself),
is described entirely in terms of the actions of those who work upon
him: he "is a gibbet for all manner of cheats and rogues to hang upon; a Bridewel [a prison], where pickpockets and rooks are set on
work and kept. . . . Gamesters knap him with a whore . . . and rooks
build in him like a tree" (p. 266).

Other *characters* illustrate Butler's conviction that all extremes are
ultimately identities — as "A Popish Priest" and "A Fanatic," or "A
Philosopher" and "A Mathematician" (the mathematician beginning "in Nonsense . . . ends in Sense, and the other [the philosopher]
quite contrary begins in Sense and ends in Nonsense" [p. 119]). Of
particular interest in this connection are the unexpected relation-
ships between the subjects of the *characters*, professional disparities
that are wittily brought into focus as a single image: thus "An
Hermetic Philosopher . . . is a Kind of Hector in Learning, that
thinks to maintain himself in Reputation by picking Quarrels with
his gentle Readers" (p. 139); "A Modern Critic" is "a Mountebank,
that is always quacking of the infirm and diseased Parts of Books, to
shew his Skill" (p. 183); the alcohol in a "Sot" is like the inner light
of a Quaker (p. 162); "A Virtuoso" is compared to (of all things) a
"Country-gentleman" (cf., Butler's "Bumpkin or Country Squire"
[p. 74]). As the squires "talk of Dogs to those that hate Hunting,
because they love it themselves; so will he of his Arts and Sciences to
those that neither know, nor care to know any Thing of them" (p.
122).

This practice of interchanging character types provided Butler
with a special satiric rhetoric which enabled him to reuse apt wit-
ticisms without the effect of repetition. The "Republican," for exam-

ple, "is a civil Fanatic . . . and as all Fanatics cheat themselves with Words, mistaking them for Things; so does he with the false Sense of Liberty" (p. 55). The "Virtuoso" "differs from a Pedant, as *Things* do from *Words;* for he uses the same Affectation in his Operations and Experiments, as the other does in Language" (p. 122). Furthermore, the practice offered additional opportunity to attack especially deserving subjects — "A Pimp Is a *Solicitor* of Love, a Whore's *Broker, Procurator* of the most serene Commonwealth of Sinners, and *Agent* for the Flesh and the Devil" (p. 235 — italics added). Such figures, demonstrating the essential unity of the various forms of human folly and villainy, suggest that Butler's penchant for analogy — "If ever a man was haunted by 'the demon of analogy,' it was he," writes Ian Jack.[7] — was in fact the natural consequence of his peculiar view of the nature of life.

Behind this single-minded treatment of the variety of human society stands that paradox noted in the second chapter: that, whereas the singleness of truth is the most difficult achievement in the world, the devising of passable alternatives to it (i.e., falsehoods) is the easiest. Falsehood "has change of faces and every one proof against all impression," Butler observed in his notebook (293:4). Like a modern psychologist, he too recognized that human beings assume roles for social or personal reasons; but he regarded this phenomenon as a cause for laughter or rebuke, rather than for understanding or sympathy. To Butler, the danger of such behavior lay not in any violation of individual integrity (though, of course, the deceived is always at the mercy of the deceiver), but in the undermining of the very structure of order in human society. The man who assumes the name, but not the virtues of, learning, piety, nobility, or justice creates a confusion that makes these virtues — rare enough to begin with — all the more inaccessible.

In pointing out this deception, Butler's *characters* seem to make only a negative claim to truth: Justice is *not* this magistrate or attorney, they say; this "Huffing Courtier" is *not* a picture of nobility. Unlike Bishop Joseph Hall, Butler offers no formal portraits of the virtues. Nevertheless, there is also a positive value in this apparently destructive outlook; for, if we are brought to see that justice is merely a judge's "profession," it is likely that we shall be on our guard against his true "calling." "As other mens harmes make us cautious, so the Miscarriages of others may make us wise," Butler observed in his notebook. "He that see's another in a wrong way, is so much nearer to the right himself . . ." (283:2).

"The Generall Temper of Mankind," Butler observed, "is nothing but a Mixture of Cheat and Folly" (276:1). Let us, therefore, consider his *characters* as portraits of deceivers and as the victims of deception (their own or another's). The victims, Butler's fools, we have noticed earlier, misunderstand their true natures because they either lack reason (the madmen and proper or "natural" fools) or misuse it (the ignorant or "artificial" fools); and, as a consequence of both causes, they bear a closer resemblance to animals or machines than to men. We have explained the general category of folly by Butler's assertion that "Men without Reason [and men who misuse it] . . . fall short of that which give's them their Being . . ." (339:3). Such a man "is not actuated by any inward principle of his own," Butler says, "but by something without him, like an engine; for he is nothing, but as he is wound up, and set a going by others" (p. 275) — by others, or by the fluctuating pressures of his own passions or "humours": but in neither case does he remain himself. The result, viewed from the outside, is usually ridiculous: the "Affected [Man]," for example, "is a Piece of Clockwork, that moves only as it is wound up and set, and not like a voluntary Agent" (p. 237); the "Sot" "has washed down his soul and pist it out . . . has swallowed his Humanity and drunk himself into a Beast, as if he had pledged *Madam Circe*. . . . He governs all his Actions by the Drink within him . . . [and having] a different Humour for every Nick his Drink rises to . . . proceeds from Ribaldry to Bawdery to Politics, Religion, and Quarreling . . ." (pp. 162 - 63). Or here is the "Fantastic," the seventeenth century dandy: "His Brain is like Quicksilver, apt to receive any Impression, but retain none. . . . He is a Cormorant, that . . . devours every Thing greedily, but it runs through him immediately" (p. 96). This wild instability of *character*, which is typical of natural folly or madness, contrasts, as we shall see, with the obsessive behavior exhibited in many types of artificial folly.

Except for those types (the Affected Man, the Sot, and the Fantastic) who seem compelled to be other than themselves, playing a role is generally a pleasureable experience; and their being pleased bears out the truth of Butler's belief that men are happiest when devising tricks that keep them from thinking of their miseries and weaknesses. It is only to the objective observer that such unnatural behavior is painful, appearing as destructive to individual integrity as innovation is to national integrity. Butler suggests this view in his use of an organic metaphor in the portrait of the "Affected Man": "All his Affectations are forced and stolen from others, and though they become some particular Persons where they grow naturally, as a

Flower does on its Stalk, he thinks they will do so by him, when they are pulled and dead. He puts Words and Language out of its ordinary Pace, and breaks it to his own Fancy, which makes it go so uneasy in a Shuffle, which it has not been used to. He delivers himself in a forced Way like one that sings with a feigned Voice beyond his natural Compass" (p. 193).

This behavior, of course, is social affectation, assuming the clothes and mannerisms of a social station higher than one's own. More interesting to Butler was what we might call professional affectation — the dabbling in some rather prestigious occupation for which one has no aptitude. But the motivation of both forms of pretense is identical: "All the Business of this World is but Diversion," the devising of "tricks" by which men manage to ignore their shortcomings (272:1). An occupation, even the most humble one, should be self-fulfilling; and, to the degree that it is, its product has value. But men literally lose themselves in their occupations with the result that their labors are fruitless. Butler's "Officer" (no more precise title will fit him) is a case in point: "Nature meant him for a man, but his office intervening put her out, and made him another thing; and as he loses his name in his authority, so he does his nature. The most predominant part in him is that in which he is something beside himself" (p. 294).

The *character* of "An Officer" explains the fatal attraction of those pursuits that Pope later satirized as "dullness," and that Butler analyzed more particularly in "A Curious Man," "A Virtuoso," "An Hermetic Philosopher," and "A Pedant." Before becoming an officer, we read, the subject "was nothing of himself, but had a great ambition to be something, and so got an office, which he stands more upon than if he had been more of himself; for having no intrinsic value he has nothing to trust to but the stamp that is set upon him, and so is necessitated to make as much of that as he can" (p. 295). Pedantry in any profession justifies itself in the same way. Butler's "Pedant" happens to be a physician: "he gives his Patients sound hard words for their Money, as cheap as he can afford; for they cost him Money and Study too, before he came by them, and he has Reason to make as much of them as he can" (p. 188).

The *little* that such pretenders make much of is their capacity to engage in "the ordinary Bus'nes, and Drudgery of the world" (288:1) — the office for which nature originally designed them, endowing them with qualities like patience and industriousness, which then become comically inappropriate to the roles they tend to assume, and cause them to succeed only in perverting their usefulness in the world. Created for slavery, such men turn whatever occupation they pretend to into drudgery. Thus the "Virtuoso," having "nothing of Nature but an Inclination . . . strives to improve [it] with Industry," which would itself be admirable "if it did not attempt [only] the greatest Difficulties . . . for he commonly slights any Thing that is plain and easy . . . and bends all his Forces against the hardest and most improbable." (p. 122).

It is merely a step from such comic forms of self-delusion (costing the pretender only an occasional embarrassment) to much more troublesome forms of deception. In fact, the only thing preventing our taking a sterner view of the fools whom we have thus far considered is Butler's assurance of their total innocence or irrationality. But the moment the virtuoso embarks upon an impossible pursuit — because it is impossible and because it permits him to say or do whatever he pleases (since no man may say he is wrong) — he deceives not only himself (or more likely not himself at all) but another. We then have what Butler (adopting the new scientific interest in motion to explain the processes of deception) called the "Mechanics of Cheat" and the "mathematical Magic of Imposture" (p. 162), of which science he is perhaps the most perceptive analyst in English.

We might, in fact, regard Butler's *characters* as a much more comprehensive and much more subtle Restoration version of the old Elizabethan coney-catching book. How does "A Ranter" — one of a wild sect of religious libertines who openly defamed the scriptures, the church, and all its conventions — practice deception? Or in what sense can the charge be levelled at "A Latitudinarian," the seventeenth century church liberal who was all for dissolving those narrow denominational differences that offered a sort of orthodox sanction for religious hypocrisy? Butler's answers to such questions in the *characters* illustrate his extraordinary interest in knavery as a conscious mental process, one that recognizes that appearances and statements exert predictable and adaptable forces. Deception is a problem in mechanics: the "Knave" is "an Engineer of Treachery, Fraud, and Perfidiousness," knowing "how to manage Matters of great Weight with very little Force, by the Advantage of his trepanning Screws" (p. 214). Butler's portraits of knavery trace the progress of this science. The "Ranter," for example, has "found out by a very strange Way of new Light, how to transform all the *Devils* into *Angels of Light*" (p. 106). When a society as sophisticated as

Restoration England has come to recognize saintliness as the mask of true wickedness, may not an unsaintly manner carry the force of virtue? Thus the "Ranter" "puts off the *old Man*, but puts it on again upon the *new one.* . . . He is but an *Hypocrite* turned the wrong Side outward; for, as the one wears his Vices within, and the other without, so when they are counter-changed the *Ranter* becomes an *Hypocrite*, and the *Hypocrite* an able *Ranter*" (pp. 106 - 07). On the other hand, the "Latitudinarian" is simply "a Kind of modest Ranter" (p. 118): he maintains that "*Christian* Liberty and *natural* Liberty may very well consist together"; and, in the event of a conflict between the two, he is prepared to give the latter ("being of the elder House") the "Precedency."

Often the line between a subject's ignorance of his motivations and his deliberate self-misrepresentation is difficult to draw. Butler's "Fanatic," for example, seems willing to endure persecution in order to conceal his unwillingness to channel his energies toward a more effective end. "He is all for suffering for Religion, but nothing for acting; for he accounts *good Works* no better than Encroachments upon the Merits of *free believing* . . ." (p. 127). Yet this character begins with Butler's observation that "the *Fanatics* of our Times are mad with too little [learning]" (p. 126); and Butler concludes by calling him "a Puppet Saint" whose "Ignorance is the dull leaden Weight that puts all his Parts in Motion" (p. 128). On the whole, it is difficult to generalize from the evidence of the *characters* to Butler's attitude toward his subjects. If his view of the "Fanatic" seems strangely ambivalent, his judgments upon similar faults in the "Sceptic" and the "Zealot" (a second version of the "Fanatic") are not: in "undervaluing that, which he cannot attain to," the sceptic "would make his Necessity appear a Virtue . . ." (p. 165); and of the zealot we are told "his Zeal is never so vehement, as when it concurs with his Interest. . . . He is very severe to other Men's Sins, that his own may pass unsuspected . . ." (p. 231).

We know from a statement in his notebook that Butler, like Dante, took a graver view of fraud than of violence: "a Cheat is worse than a Thiefe," he wrote; for the former "do's not only Rob a man of his Goodes (as a thiefe do's) but his Reputation also, and makes him Combine and take Part against himself: Steale's and convey's him, out of his Reason, and Senses . . ." (329:1). In general, the characters can be read as a demonstration of this Aristotelian view of wrongdoing. Nevertheless, Butler's moral bias should not allow us to forget his relationship to the Overburian writers and, in particular, to their

conversion of the traditional moral *character* into an occasion for witty improvisation. Butler continued this tradition by employing the
character as an intellectual exercise rather than a form of moral ex-
hortation — organizing large parts of a particular portrait around a
central image, creating an entire sketch out of contrasting conceits,
or testing the limits of ironic perspective.

For example, Butler would have found little satisfaction as an art-
ist in repeating the hackneyed anti-Catholic prejudices that he no
doubt shared as an English Protestant. He therefore begins his
character of "A Popish Priest" by taking for granted certain contemporary assumptions about the subject — about the priest's
"profession." Specifically, he assumes that every man, at least,
knows the Catholic priest's chief duty in England: infiltration of the
family in order to proselytize its women: "His Profession is to disguise himself, which he does in Sheep's-Cloathing, that is, a Lay
Habit." There is, in other words, no question about the essentially
deceptive nature of priesthood; nor is there, for once, any discrepancy between this subject's "profession" and his true calling. The
"great Question," Butler then says, is whether the "Sheep's-
Cloathing" of the priest covers a "Wolf, a Thief, or a Shepherd":
"only this is certain, that he had rather have one Sheep out of
another Man's Fold, than two out of his own. He . . . keeps his Flock
always in Hurdles, to be removed at his Pleasure; and though their
Souls be rotten or scabby with Hypocrisy, the Fleece is sure to be
sound and orthodox. He . . . always keeps the Wool, that he pulls
from the Sore, to himself" (p. 100). Wolf, thief, or shepherd? Certainly not the shepherd, we may conclude. On the other hand, is
there anything wolflike in the description of the priest's personality?
May he not be simply a shepherd in "Sheep's-Cloathing" and
nothing else? The reader may answer the "great Question" as he
pleases; the author, we might believe, considered it a purely rhetorical one. For Butler, this *character* was a form of witty play, a testing
of the validity of a cliché.

Often Butler's play is pure invention, the exercise of the imagination upon only one or two features of the subject. In the following
allusions to the "Anabaptist's" affinity for water, for example, we
notice how self-contained — how much a part of the witty allusions
themselves — is the polemical force of the *character:*

[He is] a Water-Saint, that, like a Crocodile, sees clearly in the Water, but
dully on Land.
[He lives] in two Elements like a Goose. . . .

He is contrary to a Fisher of Men; for instead of pulling them out of the water, he dips them in it.

He is a Landerer of Souls, and tries them, as Men do Witches, by Water. He dips them all under Water, but their Hands, which he holds them up by — those do still continue *Pagan*. . . .

His dipping makes him more obstinate and stiff in his Opinions, like a Piece of hot Iron, that grows hard by being quenched in cold Water.

He does not like the use of Water in his Baptism, as it falls from Heaven in Drops, but as it runs out of the Bowels of the Earth, or stands putrefying in a dirty Pond.

He chuses the coldest Time in the Year to be dipped in, to shew the Heat of his Zeal, and this renders him the more obstinate.

His Church is under the watry Government of the Moon, when she was in *Aquarius*.

He finds out Sloughs and Ditches, that are aptest for launching of an Anabaptist; for he does not christen, but launch his Vessel. (pp. 214 - 17)

The same procedure is employed in the *characters* of "A Huffing Courtier," which is defined in terms of clothing, and of "An Haranguer," which was probably inspired by William Prynne, the Puritan pamphleteer whose libelous tongue cost him both ears in the pillory. Throughout the "Haranguer," Butler plays upon both details ("His Ears have catched the Itch of his Tongue"); and the result is something closer to caricature than portraiture.

We suspect that Butler composed such pieces at great speed, dashing off the images as they came; caring little about repetition, sequence, or consistency ("A Rabble," for example, is described as a flock of sheep, a herd of swine, and the "most savage Beast in the whole World" [pp. 197 - 98]); caring only whether the imagination were pressed to its limit and thoroughly delivered. Rather than expunge or revise, Butler used superfluous imagery to prime his imagination on some new aspect of the subject. The various imperfections in the character of "An Undeserving Favourite" (pp. 206 - 09) permit us to form some idea of this working method. Because a "favorite" is literally defined by the favors he receives from his king, Butler's chief emphasis in this *character* is upon the contrast between these favors and the undeservingness of the subject. Accordingly, the opening clause defines the type as a coin, but one of "base Metal" — a counterfeit — and its sole authenticity is the impression of the king's face that it bears: "An Undeserving Favourite/Is a Piece of base Metal with the King's Stamp upon it" — adding, as if at the suggestion of the color of the base metal or the shape of the coin, this appositive: "[he is] a Fog raised by the Sun, to

obscure his own Brightness." This implied concern for the moral
reputation of the king ("the Sun") in uncharacteristic of Butler — so
much so that we wonder if he has not failed to make his intended
point. A similar difficulty appears in the next sentence — "He came
to Preferment by unworthy Offices, like one that rises with his Bum
forwards, which the Rabble hold to be fortunate." Again the point is
obscure; but, rather than delete it or even revise it, Butler makes
another attempt to state it more clearly: "He got up to Preferment
on the wrong Side, and sits as untoward in it." And then, as if still
unsatisfied with the expression of the idea, he gives us yet another
explanation. The favorite is not comfortable in his seat of favor; since
he does not deserve his place, he does not become it. Based upon
something other than worth, his elevation is merely superficial; it
fails to distinguish him above his peers: "He is raised rather above
himself than others," Butler writes, "or as base Metals are by the
Test of Lead, while Gold and Silver continue still unmoved."
Though the last figure picks up the metal imagery of the counterfeit
coin, we might well feel that "the Test of Lead" is somewhat in-
correctly applied in this context since heavy or "base Metals" would
be precipitated rather than "raised" from mixtures containing gold
or silver (as Butler more nearly suggests with the same figure in the
character of "An Ignorant Man" [p. 282]).

But this figure may also have brought to a more conscious level in
Butler's mind several other notions only faintly suggested thus far in
the *character*. One of these is the juxtaposition, from the very first
sentence, of images suggesting both sinking and rising. It is of course
in the nature of a favorite to *rise*, and we may suppose too that he is
light insofar as he lacks substantial value; but the type is also, for
Butler, essentially heavy, dull, leaden, endowed with the qualities of
ignorance rather than intelligence and wit. This paradoxical nature
of the favorite now emerges in the alchemical figure as an actual
confusion in the author's mind. Furthermore, the figure suggests a
new focus of interest in the subject. In order to show that the undeserved favorite is a counterfeit creation, Butler observes that "he is
raised rather above himself than others" (p. 207). Although this
statement indicates that undeserved favoritism does not alter the essential nature of the favored, it also suggests that it has no effect
upon the unfavored — an implication that Butler, as a case of unrecognized merit himself, would certainly have rejected. In describing metaphorically the relative effect of favors, Butler suggests,
however, the essential injustice of the situation: "Gold and Silver

continue still unmoved" — i.e., true worth goes unrecognized. We may see now that Butler seems to have been moving toward this idea from the very beginning (we notice, for instance, the increasingly distinct echoes of Shakespeare's thirty-third sonnet); but we only gradually became conscious of it. Not until the fifth sentence is it fully articulated: "He is born like a Cloud on the Air of the Prince's Favour, and keeps his Light from the rest of his People" (p. 207).

Butler's range of metaphorical reference in the *characters* is much wider than the preceding passage from "An Undeserving Favourite" indicates. Indeed, it is difficult to think of a field of learning, an activity, or a human experience that does not contribute some image or allusion to his *characters*. Much of this material is learned in nature, the product of reading, study, or attention to the complex affairs of contemporary politics, religion, and philosophy. The portrait of "A Fifth-Monarchy-Man," for instance, includes references to Perkin Warbec and Lambert Simnel, political pretenders of earlier English history; the Anabaptist leader, John of Leyden; Romulus, one of the legendary founders of Rome; the aborative insurrection and punishment of Thomas Venner and his Fifth-Monarchy-Men (1660 - 61); the fairyland monarchy of King Oberon; Aeneas' visions of the Roman Empire; Mahommed; and King Arthur. Among the philosophers mentioned in the *characters*, we find such expected names as Plato, Aristotle, Hobbes, Descartes, Bacon, and More, as well as a number of lesser-known writers on more esoteric branches of the subject — Agrippa, Cardon, Charlton, Raymond Lully, Conrad Gesner, Jacob Boehme, and Alexander Ross.

Butler may employ a scholastic distinction in a secular context — like that which compares the conversation of "An Amorist" to the intuition of an angel (p. 108) — or draw upon recent scientific investigation to develop a remark on religion or morality — as when he observes that ritual increases the force of religion in the Catholic much as a magnet draws a greater weight through a piece of iron (p. 104); or compares the Sot's way of renewing his childhood with "the *Virtuoso's* Way of making old Dogs young again" — i.e., by transfusion (pp. 161 - 62). Even Butler's puns tend to be learned — typographical, like the identification of the "Cuckold's" head with Pythagoras' letter (both are "troubled with a forked Distinction" [p. 210]); etymological, like the "Undeserving Favourite's" *honor* (it is to be understood in its "original Sense . . . which among the Ancients *(Gellius* says) signified Injury" [p. 208]); or grammatical ("A Pimp" is "a Conjunction copulative, that joins different Cases, Genders, and Persons" [p. 237]). Scriptual allusions (though rather common ones) are frequent, as are also references to the Greek classics and the Roman satirists. But, outside of an obviously literary subject like "A Small Poet," allusions to later literary figures are rare. In the last-named *character*, Butler refers to Ben Jonson and Edward Benlowes, the emblem poets; William Prynne; and perhaps Sir William Davenant. Elsewhere, the important French critic Julius Scaliger is several times mentioned, and there are references to Sylvester's translation of Du Bartas, to Chaucer's pilgrims, and to occasional recollections of characters from the plays of Jonson, Marlowe, and Shakespeare.

In marked contrast to this learned material are the allusions to popular legend, fable, and proverb, imagery of everyday life and common sense truth that Butler uses in the *characters*. Some of this material may have been recalled from his rural youth and early career at various country estates: glimpses of the wretched roads of the North Country, which appear as an analogy for the tiresome discourse of the "Tedious Man" (p. 173), references to rustic drinking customs (p. 240), and the special knowledge of farmers, hunters, and fishermen (pp. 137, 138, 241, 242). Here too is the expertise of more sophisticated games — bowls, dice, tennis, *L'Ombre*, and "Inn and Inn" — and the sights and sounds of the city: the "link-boy" who lights the dark ways (a metaphor for the self-illuminated Quaker [p. 200]); the watchman with his blunt bill speciously "chalk'd" to appear sharp (an analogy of false wit); street names like "Ram-alley" (p. 317), and "Lewkner's Lane" (p. 236); and shop signs like the "Turks Head," where Harrington's Rota Club met (p. 258), the "Dog and Partridge" in Fleet Street (p. 236), and the vintner's "bush" (p. 217).

For the modern reader, this witty application of the commonplace is probably the most memorable feature of Butler's *characters:* the Haranguer's tongue, always in motion, though to little purpose, is "like a Barber's Scissors, which are always snipping, as well when they do not cut, as when they do" (p. 99). The clothes-conscious fanatic, "sure to be earliest in the Fashion, lays out for it like the first Pease and Cherries" (p. 96); on the other hand, the knave "grows rich by the Ruin of his Neighbors, like Grass in the Streets in a great Sickness" (p. 214). One of the few generalizations we can make about such figures — aside from the obvious fact that each presents a fresh impression of Butler's actual world — is that they tend to be one-dimensional: they are merely witty illustrations rather than expressions of insight. True, the image of a luxuriant growth of grass in the street of a plague-infested city is actually quite complex; it may express desertedness, the triumph of the natural over the artificial, or the irrepressibility of the life force. For Butler, however, the value of the image is drastically restricted: he means only that knaves and grass are alike in that both flourish at the expense of men. Butler's figures collapse under any greater interpretive pressure. They are to be enjoyed simply as unexpected similitudes, wondered at, perhaps, for their perspicuity, but then dropped for the next in turn; and, since the peripheral overtones of these images are nonfunctional, we find little evidence of an associational logic that determined that next image.

Indeed, Butler's tendency to repeat images (animals, machinery, clothes) imparts a greater sense of unity to the entire collection of *characters* than is produced by the images within any single *character*. The significant patterns emerge only in broad perspective. Man is a beast — or worse — the *characters* say collectively; or man, the rational animal, is a flattering fiction — in reality, he is an automaton; or men are never what they appear to be — all practice some form of deception. These images, and their implications in Butler's thought have been mentioned in earlier chapters; but one other class of repeated imagery may yet be mentioned, that of buying and selling, the making and spending of money, and the production and consumption of commodities.

In many cases, of course, the language and imagery of commerce is called for by the middle class subjects of the *characters* ("A Shopkeeper," "A Vintner," "A Banker"), and Butler is quite adept at employing the special vocabularies of the professions and trades he describes. But we are thinking now of commerce as a metaphor: the "Small Poet" as "Haberdasher . . . with a very small Stock, and no Credit" (p. 82); the "Lawyer" as "Retailer of Justice, that uses false Lights, false Weights, and false Measures" (p. 111); and the "Astrologer" as "Retailer of Destiny, and petty Chapman to the Planets" (p. 110). It is perhaps a mistake to read any sort of economic prejudice into such imagery; to suggest, as Norma Bentley has, that Butler was an aspirant to membership in the "leisure class"[8] and hence was contemptuous of that class that he wished to, but could not, leave. True, there is a touch of this sentiment in his *character* of "A Shopkeeper": "Country Gentlemen," he says in it, "always design the least hopeful of their Children to Trades, and out of that Stock the City is supplied with that sottish Ignorance, which we see it perpetually abound with" (p. 199). It is also true that the middle class moneymakers of Butler's day were Puritan, and of course Butler was critical of the Puritans. But his criticism was directed at the spiritual pretenses of Puritanism, not at its economic philosophy — or, indirectly, at the latter only if it revealed pretense, as in this passage from the long polemical *character* of "A Hypocritical Nonconformist": "The Wealth of his Party . . . is no mean Motive to enflame his Zeal, and encourage him to use the Means, and provoke all Dangers, where such large Returns may infallibly be expected. . . . For so many and great have been the Advantages of this thriving Persecution, that the Constancy and Blood of the primitive Martyrs did not propagate the Church more, than the Money and good Creatures earned by these profitable Sufferings have done the Discipline of the modern Brethren" (p. 46).

The brand of commerce was for Butler not a social, but an ethical, stigma. "Many excellent Persons have been born and lived in the City," he says in the *character* of "A City-Wit"; but "there are very few such that have been bred there, though they come from all Parts and Families of the Nation; for Wit is not the Practice of the Place, and a London Student is like an *University* Merchant" (p. 226). Butler's *characters* suggest that the men of commerce were themselves aware of what they had done to trade. The "Shopkeeper," for example, is ashamed of his occupation; he regards it as neither a profession, nor a calling, but as "a *Mystery*"; and Butler adds that "rightly interpreted [that mystery] signifies only this — That as all *Turks* are Tradesmen, even so all Tradesmen are Turks" (p. 199).

CHAPTER 6

The Vogue of Hudibras: *Conclusion*

BECAUSE Butler published little in his lifetime and acknowledged only a portion of that, an assessment of his significance must, in large part, be an account of the popularity and influence of *Hudibras* and its satiric methods. Butler's reputation as a thinker — the aspect of his work that has interested us in this study — has grown slowly, governed, as it has been, by the gradual publication of the notebook materials. As for his characters, which could have made a real contribution to the rhetoric of prose satire, their publication in 1759 came at a time when the form had already become a historical curiosity and when satire itself had fallen into decline. But the voice of *Hudibras*, or at least something recognizable as an impersonation of that voice, remained as a very audible echo in satiric verse throughout the Restoration and the following century. A borrowed rhyme here, a phrase there, like the following from Swift's "Epistle to a Lady" — "You, like some acute Philosopher, /Ev'ry Fault have drawn a Gloss over" — or, recalling the "argument" of Butler's opening canto, these lines from Byron's much later production, *Don Juan* — "Carelessly I sing, /But Phoebus lends me now and then a string, /With which I still can harp, and carp, and fiddle, /. . . . But now I choose to break off in the middle" — such echoes (however conscious) do not, of course, constitute imitation. Swift and Byron — though they each may have found certain metrical tricks in Butler — were themselves originals. The great vogue of hudibrastic imitation appears in a much less distinguished roster of anonymous hacks, second rate poetasters, and novices who hoped to gain the public's attention by reworking the vein of the most popular poem of the Restoration.

Perhaps the most commonly imitated feature of *Hudibras* is its rough octosyllabic meter, the doggeral "hudibrastic" couplet. It is, of course, impossible to establish a precedent with Butler's practice

in the meter. Milton employed tetrameter couplets in *L'Allegro* and
Il Penseroso; Andrew Marvell used them in "The Garden" and "To
His Coy Mistress"; and their value as a vehicle for all sorts of hit-
and-run satiric attacks must have extended through broadside
ballads and lampoons back to the Middle Ages. Butler made
something new of this form, however, as the author of the
anonymous imitation entitled *Pendragon; or the Carpet Knight* indicated in 1698: *Hudibras* "stands upon Four Feet," he wrote; "but
its Liberties and Privileges are unbounded; and those Four Feet are,
I think, by no means obliged to be but Eight Syllables; for in place of
the Last, it is a part of its Excellency some times to have Two, Three,
or Four Syllables (like so many Claws) crowded into the Time of One
Foot. The Duple and Triple *Rhyme,* in some other *Poetry* much
blamable, are Beauties in this. . . ."[1] This commentator only begins
to touch on the art of Butler's couplets; what probably attracted him
and his fellow imitators was the apparent carelessness of the form,
the license which it offered for unbounded "Liberties and
Privileges" — always a condition of frequent literary imitation.
Nevertheless, the meter of *Hudibras* was closely enough imitated
that in 1715 the editors of the *Posthumous Works* of Butler were
either fooled themselves or succeeded in fooling the reading public
of the day by including in the edition a number of works in
hudibrastics not written by Butler. By 1700, according to Edward
Ames Richard's bibliography of hudibrastic verse, twenty-five works
had been published in the meter, and Richard P. Bond's "Register of
Burlesque Poems" lists an additional fifty-six titles before 1750.

Two other features of hudibrastic imitation — the reuse of Butler's
quixotic fable and the employment of his peculiar satiric method —
have been thoroughly canvassed by Richards and Bond, and shall
not concern us here. We can, however, take notice of one other
aspect of hudibrastic influence that these more comprehensive surveys have had to ignore. I refer to the occurrence in satiric narratives
after 1660 of the pattern of Butler's opening lines in *Hudibras,*
perhaps the most memorable feature of the poem — that is, the
"When . . . When . . . When . . . Then . . ." formula or some variation
of it. Such a statement implies what cannot, of course, be positively
asserted: that Butler invented the pattern. It is surprising that we
cannot find so natural an organizing device *(cum . . . tum . . .* in
Latin) among the illustrations of traditional schemes in the rhetorical
handbooks of the period. Chaucer used a simplified form of it at the
beginning of the "Prologue" to the *Canterbury Tales* ("Whan that

Aprille with his shoures soote . . . Whan Zephirus eek with his sweete breeth . . . Thanne longen folk to goon on pilgrimages"); there is a suggestion of it in the opening of the "Prologue" to Langland's *Piers Plowman* ("In a somer seson whan soft was the sonne . . . Thann gan I to meten a merueilouse sweuene"); and it appears frequently and with interesting variations in Shakespeare's sonnets.

In none of these analogues, however, do the words "when" and "then" carry much temporal significance: they function rhetorically, and intransitively, as it were, as a convenient way of expressing the relationship between cause and effect or between motive and action. Butler's use of the words is insistently and transitively temporal, however. "*When* civil fury first grew high" is a metaphor for "in the 1640's" or, as Butler stated on his title page, "in the time of the late Wars"; and "*Then* did Sir Knight abandon dwelling" refers to the same time. The viewpoint is emphatically retrospective, like the "Once upon a time" of a fairytale, or — more probably the case — the "Sithen the seige was ceased" of some romance. In other words, Butler's formulaic opening is an integral part of the rhetoric of burlesque romance; and it may have been so used before it appeared in *Hudibras* since "The Authors Mock-Song to Marke Anthony," published in 1647 and attributed to Butler's good friend John Cleveland, suggests this fact:

> When as the Night-raven sung Pluto's Mattins,
> And *Cerberus* cried three Amens at a hould;
> When night-wandring Witches put on their pattins,
> Midnight as darke as their faces are fould,
>   Then did the Furies doome
>   That my night-mare should come.[2]

Whatever the source of this temporal pattern, its frequency in burlesque and satire written after the appearance of *Hudibras* strongly suggests its close dependence upon Butler's poem. Very likely, since it was the most easily imitated feature of Butler's style, it recommended itself to the novice. Here, for instance, is the first published work of the later Platonic enthusiast John Norris, a burlesque called "A Murnival of Knaves," which appeared in 1683:

> When that the poor oppressed *Press*
> Groan'd under the *Cacoethes*
> Of Scribling; when *Baboon* and *Pug*
> Skirmisht in Paper-Dialogue;

> When Vile *Tom'sson* did disenbogue
> At one another *Ruffian*, *Rogue*,
> Profligate *Villain*, Fidler, Knave,
> *Buffoon* and *Rascal*, rail and rave
> In such foul terms as these; a Pack
> Enuf to break a *Porters* back,
> Or sham at th' sharpest scolding rate
> The *Wastecoteers* of *Beline's-gate:*
> When one of these loose *Pamphleteers*
> Was very near losing his Ears,
> And did through *Wood-loop-hole* survey
> The Market on a welcome day;
> Nay, had he not begg'd off close-keeping,
> And Fine, good faith, had paid for's peeping:
> Then 'twas. (ll. 1 - 19)

Clearly, Norris was not a Butler: he was uncomfortably cramped in hudibrastics (the roomy Pindarick was to become his favorite mode of expression), and his wit is hackneyed ("oppressed *Press*") and humorless (though later he does manage to rhyme "*Sister*" with "kist her"). More in the spirit of *Hudibras* are four eighteenth century burlesques by Butler's best known imitator, Ned Ward (1667 - 1731): *Hudibras Redivivius* (1705), *Englands Reformation From the time of King Henry The VIIIth To the End of Oates's Plot* (1710), *Vulgus Britannicus* (1710), and *British Wonders* (1717). All exemplify the hudibrastic opening, but *England's Reformation* comes closest perhaps to the satiric texture of Ward's model:

> When Old King *Harry* Youthful grew,
> As Eagles do, or Hawks in Mew,
> And did in spite of *Pope* and *Fate*,
> Behead, Ripp, and Repudiate
> Those too-too long liv'd things his Wives,
> With Axes, Bills, and Midwives Knives:
> When he the Papal Power rejected,
> And from the Church the Realm Dissected
> And in the great St. *PETERS* stead
> Proclaim'd himself the Churches Head.
> When he his Ancient *Queen* forsook,
> And Buxom *Anna Bollen* took,
> Then in the *Noddle* of the Nation
> He bred the Maggot *Reformation*.[3]

Ward's three other specimens illustrate a recurring modification of Butler's burlesque pattern — the blending with it of elements of the more authentically heroic opening of Dryden's *Absalom and Achitophel* ("In pious times, e'r Priest-craft did begin"). Ward's *Vulgus Britannicus*, for instance, begins —

> In Spiteful Times when *Humane Folly*,
> Discourag'd all that's Good and Holy;
> When *Peace* and *Truth* were out of Season,
> And *Zeal* had got the start of *Reason*[4] —

and in 1723, an anonymous satire entitled *The Pettifoggers* (a subject Butler would certainly have approved) brought *Absalom and Achitophel* and *Hudibras* even more closely together by setting Butler's "when" in a mythical golden age of freedom:

> In ancient Days, when Times were good,
> And Men lov'd Peace and Neighborhood;
> When all with one another bore,
> None were deem'd either Rogue or Whore;
>
> . . . .
>
> Then was Old *England* free, at least,
> From Lawyers as from Rav'nous Beast.[5]

Apparently, Dryden's more varied sequence of temporal states soon became a standard feature of the hudibrastic opening. Thus in 1698, an octosyllabic satire entitled *The Progress* (attributed to Henry Mildmay) sustained a series of temporal adverbs and prepositions (including "In former days . . . When honesty no crime was thought . . . Ere tailor's yards were scepters made;/Before each coffee club durst prate . . .") for fifty-nine lines before at last concluding "I say, ere all these things befell,/Which now long since, no tongue can tell;/Then were the Golden Days, if any."[6] Clearly, *The Progress* establishes some sort of record in the use of the device.

What we have called the "retrospective" note of Butler's opening of *Hudibras* is missing in many of these imitations of the poem, and its absence accounts for much of the difference between them and their model. Edward Ames Richards makes the same point when he describes one of the moods of *Hudibras* as "a satiric song of victory." "One might infer," he says, "that Dissent and Presbyterianism had been wiped out in 1660."[7] Butler's confidence in this defeat meant that Puritanism was no longer *his* enemy, that he could escape the narrow bitterness of party satire, broaden his satiric perspective, and freely indulge his inventiveness. In short, victory made ridiculing the Puritans fun. Most hudibrastic imitations, however, were written in the heat of party strife. They tend, therefore, to be defensive, narrowly doctrinaire, and too preoccupied with the pressing affairs of the moment to permit the witty invention which everywhere pervades Butler's poem. Hastily thrown together, they manage at best to convey only the raciness of their original — and that, as it were, is by necessity rather than choice. Norris' *Murnival of Knaves*, the first of the imitative openings cited in this chapter, was published in June 1683 as a reaction to the abortive Whig attack that same month upon Charles II, the so-called Rye House Plot. For Norris, therefore, "When . . . When . . . Then" refers to the present; the sole function of the device was to announce the fact that its author was on the right side — on Butler's side. Indeed, as Edward Ames Richards suggests, the periodic emergence of hudibrastic imitation serves as an index of the rise of Puritanism, Dissent, Catholicism — and, for that matter, any threat to the existing establishment.

Thus in England, Thomas D'Urfey (1653 - 1723), best known for a compilation of songs entitled *Pills to Purge Melancholy*, published during the year Butler died a continuation of the adventures of Hudibras and Ralph called *Butler's Ghost*, a work of Tory propaganda that plays upon the parallel between political affairs in 1680 and the 1640's.[8] Just before he died, Butler himself, it will be recalled, planned to release an old, hitherto unpublished prose tract, *The Case of King Charles I Truly Stated*, for this purpose, and two years later, Dryden responded to the same threat with *Absalom and Achitophel*. Hudibrastics were again pressed into service at the time of the English Settlement, in D'Urfey's *Collin's Walk* (1690); during the Jacobite threat, in the anonymous *Pendragon, or the Carpet Knight;* at the time of the settlement of the national church in Scotland, in *A Mock Poem, upon the Expedition of the Highland-host . . . 1678* by William Cleland; and at the rise of Methodism, in the anonymous attack upon the preacher George Whitefield entitled *The Methodists*.

Of course, not all political satire in the eighteenth century was hudibrastic; in Britain, the idiom competed with the more disciplined heroic couplet. In America, however, this competition was less apparent. We might well imagine that Americans found the satiric voices of Dryden or Pope far too aristocratic for their tastes; Butler's, on the other hand, must have seemed like one of the proletariat. Notwithstanding its author's loyalist and conservative attitudes, *Hudibras* laughingly reassured the American patriots that the aristocratic traditions they had cast off were indeed absurd, and to such a voice they would have listened with complete understanding. For this reason, as Elizabeth Cook indicates, "the native [American] satiric verse more often followed Butler's *Hudibras*" than the works of their more immediate contemporaries.[9] Bruce Granger counts "no fewer than seventy-seven Hudibrastic poems treating of matters political . . . in America,"[10] and to these could be added scores of minor works — songs, ballads, elegies, and the like — that reveal Butler's influence one way or another.

At least a part of the currency of hudibrastics in America may be attributed to the proprietary care given the form by John Trumbull, Butler's most eminent American imitator, whose own *M'Fingal*, completed in 1782, popularized the style. Of all the imitations mentioned thus far, *M'Fingal* is perhaps the only one that can be called an artistic achievement in its own right, and it may be significant that Trumbull is one of the few imitators of *Hudibras* who did not begin by attempting to duplicate his model. His own artistic integrity and his respect for *Hudibras* as an inimitable original did not permit the sort of slavish imitation we have been considering. "The Critical Reader," he wrote, "will discern that I have rather proposed to myself Swift & Churchill as models in my Hudibrastic writings, than the Author of Hudibras. I have sometimes had Butler's manner in my eye, for a few lines, but was soon forced to quit it. Indeed his kind of wit & the oddity of his Comparisons was in my Opinion never well imitated by any man, nor ever will be."[11] This statement does not say that the presence of *Hudibras* is not to be felt in the poem; a glance at the opening lines of the first canto of *M'Fingal* dispells that notion:

> WHEN YANKIES, skill'd in martial rule,
> First put the British troops to school;
> Instructed them in warlike trade,
> And new manoeuvres of parade;
> The true war-dance of Yanky-reels,
> And manual exercise of heels;
>
> . . . .
>
> From Boston, in his best array,
> Great 'Squire M'Fingal took his way,
> And graced with ensigns of renown,
> Steer'd homeward to his native town.[12]

Here again is the familiar "when" clause, out of which the peripatetic hero makes his way. But the temporal pattern is only implicit, and there is little attempt to reproduce Butler's rhyme effects. M'Fingal's burlesque credentials are solid: he is a Scot, and a clairvoyant (Trumbull took the name from the Ossianic pseudoepic *Fingal* by James Macpherson). But the hero does not remain true to his original principles; he becomes a high-churchman and a loyal king's man who turns his clairvoyance to loyalist prophecies which his patriotic countrymen force him to retract. The differences between *Hudibras* and *M'Fingal* may be located in the great social and political revolutions that had occurred in the century separating Butler from Trumbull; and it is interesting to watch the American adapt the older satiric devices to new purposes. At the same time, we must agree with Edward Ames Richards "that *M'Fingal* is a perfect justification of the fears and scorn expressed by Butler. . . . For it exhibits Dissent in its own self-contained society, with its own conventions, with the desire and the power to look askance at other forms of religious and political propriety. The wheel turns slowly, but it turns."[13]

Society expects us to undervalue imitations and to honor originals. Let us conclude with the assurance that we have performed this obligation for Butler. We must, however, since our original is *Hudibras,* guard against complacency in this action; for if there is one overriding concern in Butler's work, it is the exposure of self-delusion, of saying what we do not really believe. That *Hudibras,* then, should be the subject of such petty dishonesty, that we should attempt here to make extravagant claims about its place in our literature, would be richly ironic. Butler could have turned such an effort to satiric capital in a *character* of "A Modern Critic of *Hudibras*": "He is one who has learned that opinion in unfamiliar matters passes most easily . . . ," it might begin. Samuel Pepys, after two attempts to appreciate Butler's poem, confessed in his diary that he simply did not "see enough where the wit lies." If Pepys had the courage to say as much in public, his opinion deserves our respect, for, before anything else, *Hudibras* demands an honest response from its readers.

In our own time, Butler's poem has received such a response from its most recent commentator. Earl Miner, in a chapter entitled "Hating Our Physician" (the satirist is our physician, and, as Butler observed in his notebook, "People can never endure those, that seeke to recover them from their deare Dotage"), describes *Hudibras* as "the worst great poem in the language," and Butler as "indisputably one of the worst as well as one of the great poets in the language."[14] Although Professor Miner's study appeared too late for consideration in the present volume, we may take pleasure in its general consistency with a number of our own views of Butler, not the least of which is this concluding evaluation of the poem and its author: "worst" *and* "great." Here is the honesty that Butler demands in our criticism of *Hudibras*. Miner refuses to ignore (as we all must) the "messiness" of the poem and the ignominy of its ideas — its sheer quantity of ugliness. But, then, if we read Butler patiently, he does not let us ignore the ugliness — forces us even to consent to the integrity of his own vision of it. We must agree with Professor Miner that there is something terrible in this sort of greatness.[15]

We must, then, also assume that Butler was aware of the ugliness of *Hudibras*. The poem presents itself as a calculated reaction to the idea of "great" literature, to a tradition of "classic" norms, of literature as the paradigm of humanness, the vehicle of a viable past. A poem in a tradition presents itself in a line of succession from works that precede it, and it begins with an assurance of the usefulness of those works to itself. Tradition creates a space in which a new work can locate itself. It furnishes a system of meaning, a model of artistic expectations, and it imposes upon the poet a "voice" through which he utters not whatever he pleases, nor even everything his integrity dictates, but only what is pertinent to a grand enterprise. In effect, tradition *re-places* the poet.

Our earlier discussion of Butler's literary criticism — in particular, his repudiation of established norms as disguises of human weakness — makes it clear that he would have had little reason to think of himself as a poet in a tradition — not even in a tradition of burlesque, as we demonstrated in Chapter 3 with the help of Richmond Bond's scheme of burlesque forms. Of course, *Hudibras* makes ironic reference to earlier literature; this is the detritus of tradition that makes up much of the "mess" of the poem. But its primary reference, as we noticed in its retrospective opening lines, is to the real world. *Hudibras*, then, declines a place in the tradition — literally *dis-places* itself — and in doing so forces the reader to repudiate tradition because the works it sanctions do not imitate life as it is, and because it cannot sanction a work that uncompromisingly does imitate it as it is. In rejecting the "voice" imposed by tradition, Butler made his own integrity the medium of *Hudibras*. It is interesting to speculate whether this may not be the reason that in his lifetime the title of his poem was attached to his own name — Hudibras Butler.

Butler probably paid little attention to the famous controversy of his time between the defenders of ancient and modern learning; as any number of his *characters* indicate, he regarded ancient tradition and modern science alike as avenues of escape from the unpleasant facts of human experience. From our vantage point, however, Butler appears as the first important literary "Modern," using this word now as a descriptive rather than an evaluative term. Even with this qualification, however, we are likely to be unhappy with the characterization of Butler as a Modern. It appears to ignore the fact that his foremost admirers in the next generation were the Modern-baiting Scriblerians, men like Swift, and Pope, and John Garth; and, of course, it condemns him by association with their enemies, Thomas Hobbes, William Wotten, and Richard Bentley — not to mention Swift's Grub-Street narrator of *The Tale of a Tub*, and the morose (dare we say "messy"?) spider of his *Battle of the Books*. We may now see that it was to Butler's credit that he gained his most distinguished apostles from hostile quarters, and that his greatest value is still to teach us that human distinctions are at bottom self-serving. The perfect integrity of his vision of human weakness and the totality of his contempt for it separates only himself from all the others.

Notes and References

Chapter One

1. Samuel Johnson, *Lives of the English Poets* (London, 1954), I, 119.
2. E. S. de Beer, "The Later Life of Samuel Butler," *Review of English Studies*, IV (1928), 159. The "Astry Life" was reprinted in Zachary Grey's 1744 edition of *Hudibras*. Johnson also had access to the biographical information later published in Treadway Russell Nash's 1793 edition of the poem.
3. See John Wilders, Introduction, *Hudibras* (Oxford, 1967), p. xiii.
4. Johnson, p. 115.
5. The most detailed account of Butler's childhood is René Lamar's "Du nouveau sur l'auteur d'"Hudibras': Samuel Butler en Worcestershire," *La Revue Anglo-Américaine*, I (1924), 213 - 27. See also R. M. Wilding, "The Date of Samuel Butler's Baptism," *Review of English Studies*, XVII (1966), 174 - 77.
6. See Michael Wilding, "Samuel Butler at Barbourne," *Notes and Queries*, XIII (1966), 17.
7. *Ibid.*, p. 15. The elder Butler's will is quoted from Wilders, p. xvi.
8. See René Lamar, "Samuel Butler à l'École du Roi," *Etudes anglaises*, V (1952), 17 - 24.
9. Michael Wilding, p. 17.
10. Wilders, p. xvii.
11. In her doctoral dissertation, "Hudibras Butler" (Syracuse University, 1944), Norma E. Bentley notes that "Butler mentions Seldon only once in the *Manuscript Commonplace Book*" (pp. 39 - 40). See also A. R. Waller's edition of Butler's *Characters and Passages from Note-Books* (Cambridge, 1908), p. 307:3. The latter volume is my source, throughout this study, of Butler's prose notebook material. Specific passages are identified by page and paragraph.
12. John Aubrey, *Brief Lives*, edited by Andrew Clark (Oxford, 1898), I, 135.
13. Hardin Craig, "*Hudibras*, Part I, and the Politics of 1647," in *The*

Manly Anniversary Studies in Language and Literature (Chicago, 1923), pp. 145 - 55.

14. Unless otherwise indicated, Wilders' edition of *Hudibras* (Oxford, 1967) is my source for all quotations from the poem. They are normally parenthetically identified by part, canto, and line.

15. Ricardo Quintana, "The Butler-Oxenden Correspondence," *Modern Language Notes*, XLVIII (1933), 3. Both letters are quoted in Appendix A of Wilders' edition of *Hudibras*.

16. *Ibid.*, p. 4.

17. *Ibid.*, p. 7. Wilders (p. xlvi) has discovered literary allusions in Part I of the poem to works that were published after the Restoration.

18. Aubrey, vol. I, pp. 174 - 75.

19. *Ibid.*, I, 136. See also Wilders, p. xviii.

20. My source for all Butler's *characters* is *Samuel Butler 1612 - 1680: Characters*, edited by Charles W. Daves (Cleveland, 1970). The three quoted passages are to be found on pp. 113, 102, and 114. Hereafter page references to the *characters* are cited parenthetically in the text. On Butler's relation to the law, see René Lamar, "Samuel Butler et la Justice de son Temps," *Etudes anglaises*, VII (1954), 271 - 79.

21. Quintana, p. 4.

22. *Satires and Miscellaneous Poetry and Prose*, edited by René Lamar (Cambridge, 1928), p. 366. All six works, except Lord Roos' *Answer*, are included in this edition.

23. Prynne is mentioned by name in the mock-invocation to *Hudibras* (I, i, 640) and elsewhere in the poem, and in the *characters* (note particularly the character of "An Haranguer").

24. Details of the scandal are given by J. Milton French in *The Life Records of John Milton* (New Brunswick, 1958), V, 11 - 15. See also C. J. Hindle, "A Broadside by Samuel Butler," *Times Literary Supplement*, March 21, 1936, p. 244.

25. Paul Bunyan Anderson argues impressively for Butler's authorship of two additional related works published in 1660: *The Character of the Rump*, and *The Censure of the Rota Upon Mr. Milton's Book, Entituled, A Ready and Easie way to Establish a Free Commonwealth*. See "Anonymous Critic of Milton: Richard Leigh? or Butler?" *Studies in Philology*, XLIV (1947), 504 - 18. The suggestion that Butler produced much besides *Hudibras* that did not originally bear his name is strengthened by a comment on libel and lampoons in his notebook: these, he wrote, "Spread like News, and all Pretenders to wit and Intelligence hold it a Disparagment to their Parts to be unfurnished of them, in which all men seem to bee so much concernd, that nothing passes so safely under the Rose, and Seal of Secresy (for though they pass through so many hands, the Right Authors are seldom or never Discoverd)" (431:5). The authorship of *Hudibras* was, of course, quickly "discoverd."

26. Unless otherwise noted, my source of Butler's minor verse is the sec-

ond volume of *The Poetical Works of Samuel Butler* (New York, 1854) — hereafter identified as *P. W.*

27. Peter Cunningham, "The Author of Hudibras at Ludlow Castle," *Notes and Queries*, 1st ser., V (1852), 5 - 6.

28. Pepys' diary entry is dated February 6, 1663.

29. Wilders, pp. liv - lv.

30. *Ibid.*, p. xlvii.

31. James L. Thorson, "The Publication of *Hudibras*," *Papers of the Bibliographical Society of America*, LX (1966), 423, 432 - 34.

32. De Beer, p. 164. Aubrey (vol. I, p. 136) mentions that the king and Lord Chancellor Hyde "both promised him great matters, but to this day he haz got *no* employment. . . .

33. Anthony à Wood, *Athenae Oxonienses*, edited by Philip Bliss (London, 1817), III, 875.

34. The letter is reprinted in *Satires and Miscellaneous Poetry and Prose*, p. 399. Aubrey (vol. I, p. 136) notes that Butler "maried a good jointuresse . . . by which meanes he lives comfortably."

35. Thyer's prefatory remarks on the *characters* (first printed in the *Genuine Remains*) are reprinted in Waller's edition of *Characters and Passages from Note-Books*, p. 481.

36. A. H. de Quehen, "Editing Butler's Manuscripts" in *Editing Seventeenth-Century Prose*, edited by D. I. B. Smith (Toronto, 1972).

37. Howard's place in "To a Bad Poet" is suggested by a rhyme: "When I would praise an author, the untoward/Damn'd sense, says *Virgil*, but the rhyme _____" (ll. 21 - 22, *P. W.*), and by Butler's statement in the "Palinode" that he has "Thrice humbly thus, in form of paper," written on Howard. All four poems (the last under the title "Satire on Rhyme") are included in the *Genuine Remains*.

38. Marjorie Hope Nicolson, *Pepys' Diary and the New Science* (Charlottesville, 1965), pp. 152, 157.

39. See Norma E. Bentley, "Hudibras Butler Abroad," *Modern Language Notes*, XL (1945), 254 - 59.

40. Wilders, p. xx.

41. De Beer, p. 163.

42. Wood, vol. IV, p. 209. Butler may also at this time have published *The Transposer Rehears'd: or the Fifth Act of Mr. Baye's Play* (1673), one of several replies to Marvell's *The Rehearsal Transposed*. See Anderson, pp. 504 - 18.

43. Quoted by De Beer, p. 162.

44. Prynne's two anti-Quaker tracts, *The Quakers Unmasked* (mentioned in the letter assigned to Prynne), and *A new discovery of some Romish emissaries*, appeared in 1655 and 1656, the first being reissued in 1664.

45. Nicolson, pp. 151 - 52. For the date of composition of the "Epistle to Sidrophel," see Wilders, p. xlvii.

46. The injunction is reprinted by Jan Veldkamp, in *Samuel Butler: The*

Author of Hudibras (Hilversum, 1923), pp. 22 - 23. A similar injunction had been issued to Butler on November 23 or 24, 1663, according to De Beer, p. 162.
    47. Wilders, p. lvi.
    48. De Beer, p. 165.
    49. *Ibid.*
    50. H. F. Brooks, "Gift to Samuel Butler," *Times Literary Supplement,* July 6, 1940, p. 327.
    51. "The Parish of St. Paul Covent Garden," in *Survey of London,* edited by F. H. W. Sheppard (London, 1970), XXXVII, 183.
    52. Aubrey, vol. I, p. 136.
    53. Bentley, "Hudibras Butler," p. 11. See also Miss Bentley's article "Another Butler Manuscript," *Modern Philology,* XLIV (1948), 132 - 35.
    54. De Quehen, p. 71.
    55. *Ibid.,* pp. 72, 82. The holograph manuscript contains even the "lost" folio material that was first printed in *The London Magazine* (1825 - 26). See Josephine Bauer, "Some Verse Fragments and Prose *Characters* by Samuel Butler Not Included in the Complete Works," *Modern Philology,* XLV (1948), 160 - 68.
    56. Johnson, vol. I, p. 122.
    57. De Quehen, p. 74. Compare, as illustrations of this refining process, pp. 454:3, 431:2, and 275:1 in the notebook materials published by Waller.
    58. De Quehen, pp. 91 - 92.
    59. Bauer, p. 162.

Chapter Two

    1. Ricardo Quintana, "Samuel Butler: A Restoration Figure in a Modern Light," *English Literary History,* XVIII (1951), 14 - 15.
    2. Jackson I. Cope, *Joseph Glanvill: Anglican Apologist* (St. Louis, 1956), p. 110.
    3. Don Cameron Allen, *The Legend of Noah: Renaissance Rationalism in Art, Science, and Letters* (Urbana, 1963), p. 23.
    4. Butler's *Commonplace Book,* pp. 4a and b. Quoted by Bentley in "Hudibras Butler," p. 199.
    5. Paul Fussell, *The Rhetorical World of Augustan Humanism* (Oxford, 1965), p. 232.
    6. *Ibid.,* p. 222.
    7. Alexander C. Spence, whose facsimile text of *The Elephant in the Moon* I am using here, has dated the octosyllabic version of the satire as "1676, or perhaps a little earlier." See *Samuel Butler: Three Poems* (Los Angeles, 1961), p. iv. But Nicolson (pp. 151 - 52) suggests more convincingly that the reference to Stubbe in the octosyllabic version was an interpolation from the "long verse" version by Robert Thyer, Butler's first editor.
    8. Nicolson has identified several of the speakers in the satire as members

of the Royal Society. See also Sv. Bruun, "Who's Who in Samuel Butler's *The Elephant in the Moon,*" *English Studies,* L (1969), 381 - 89.

9. Thomas Hobbes, "The Answer to D'Avenant," in *Critical Essays of the Seventeenth Century,* edited by J. E. Spingarn (Oxford, 1908), II, 56.

10. Quintana, "Samuel Butler," p. 28.

11. "Lines on Tentative Subjects," *Satires and Miscellaneous Verse and Prose,* p. 441.

12. Fussell, p. 172.

13. Butler's Commonplace Book, p. 52a, quoted by Bentley in "Hudibras Butler," p. 91.

14. *Ibid.,* p. 53b, quoted by Bentley, "Hudibras Butler," p. 91.

15. Seventeenth century Anglican rationalism is clearly defined by Philip Harth in *Swift and Anglican Rationalism* (Chicago, 1961).

16. Bentley, "Hudibras Butler," p. 120; de Quehen, p. 83.

17. Butler's Commonplace Book, p. 51a, quoted by Bentley, "Hudibras Butler," p. 120.

Chapter Three

1. Wilders, Commentary, *Hudibras,* pp. 450 - 51.

2. See Ian Jack, *Augustan Satire: Intention and Idiom in English Poetry: 1660 - 1750* (Oxford, 1952), pp. 15 - 16. See also G. W. Duffett, "The Name 'Hudibras,' " *Notes and Queries,* IX (1935), 96.

3. See Wilders, Commentary, p. 330.

4. Butler's letter to Oxenden, *Ibid.,* pp. 450 - 51.

5. Veldkamp studies Butler's relation to Cervantes and Rabelais in detail. See his chapters IV and V.

6. See the analysis of Ralph by W. O. S. Sutherland, Jr., *The Art of the Satirist* (Austin, 1965), pp. 65 - 66.

7. Wilders, Commentary, p. 451.

8. Wilders includes the most important identifications from the "Key" in his commentary, *Ibid.,* pp. 330, 341.

9. Craig, pp. 151 - 53.

10. W. S. Miller, "The Allegory in Part I of *Hudibras,*" *Huntington Library Quarterly,* XXI (1958), 326.

11. *Ibid.* At the end of her doctoral dissertation, Norma Bentley sketches a psychological interpretation of *Hudibras* that arrives at a point not too far from Miller's conclusion. See "Hudibras Butler," pp. 202 - 12.

12. Wilders, Introduction, pp. xliv - xlvi.

13. Miller, p. 328.

14. Alvin Kernan, *The Plot of Satire* (New Haven, 1965), p. 4.

15. *Ibid.,* p. 3.

16. *Ibid.,* p. 4.

17. Richmond P. Bond, *English Burlesque Poetry: 1700 - 1750* (Cambridge, Mass., 1932), p. 5.

18. *Ibid.*, p. 4.

19. *Ibid.*, p. 6.

20. James Sutherland, *English Literature of the Late Seventeenth Century* (Oxford, 1969), p. 160.

21. Wilders, Introduction, p. xxxv.

22. Edward Ames Richards, *Hudibras in the Burlesque Tradition* (New York, 1937), pp. x, 121.

23. Ruth Nevo, *The Dial of Virtue* (Princeton, 1963), pp. 188, 189.

24. Bond, p. 5.

25. Jack, pp. 23 - 24, 46.

26. Quoted by Karl Shapiro and Robert Benn in *A Prosody Handbook* (New York, 1965), p. 188.

27. Nevo, p. 192.

28. *The Spectator*, no. 59 (May 8, 1711); no. 60 (May 9, 1711).

29. Alexander Pope, *Peri Bathous*, in *The Art of Sinking in Poetry*, edited by Edna Leake Steeves, Chapter XII (New York, 1952).

30. Kernan, p. 171.

31. "Poetical Thesarus," *Satires and Miscellaneous Poetry and Prose*, p. 224.

32. *Ibid.*, p. 233.

33. W. O. S. Sutherland, Jr. argues for such a change in *The Art of the Satirist*, pp. 67 - 68.

34. *The Diary of Thomas Burton, Esq.*, quoted by Bentley, "Hudibras Butler," p. 192.

35. W. O. S. Sutherland, Jr., p. 71.

Chapter Four

1. The search for historical counterparts to characters in the satire has not ended: see, e.g., Joseph T. Curtiss, "Butler's *Sidrophel*," *Publications of the Modern Language Association*, XLIV (1929), 1066 - 78. For allegorical interpretations, see Craig; Ellen Douglass Leyburn, "*Hudibras* Considered as Satiric Allegory," in *Satiric Allegory: Mirror of Man* (New Haven, 1956), pp. 37 - 52; and Miller. Wilders' introduction to the poem provides a useful discussion of Butler's ideas; his commentary on the text is largely historical, however.

2. Cf. Ian Jack's interpretation of *Hudibras* as a satire on hypocrisy in *Augustan Satire*. Discussion of the contents of Butler's notebook is provided by Dan Gibson, Jr., "Samuel Butler," in *Seventeenth Century Studies*, edited by Robert Shafer (Princeton, 1933); Quintana, "Samuel Butler: A Restoration Figure in a Modern Light"; and Bentley "Hudibras Butler."

3. The "satire on man" is discussed by Bertrand A. Goldgar, "Satires on Man and 'The Dignity of Human Nature,'" *Publications of the Modern*

Language Association, LXXX (1965), 535 - 41; and by W. B. Carnochan, *Lemuel Gulliver's Mirror for Man* (Berkeley, 1968).

4. George Boas, *The Happy Beast in French Thought of the Seventeenth Century* (Baltimore, 1933). Additional information on theriophily may be found in the following Swift studies: Elizabeth Barker, "Giovanni Battista Gelli's *Circe* and Jonathan Swift," *Cesare Barbieri Courier,* II (1959), 3 - 15; R. S. Crane, "The Houyhnhnms, the Yahoos, and the History of Ideas," in *Reason and the Imagination: Studies in the History of Ideas 1600 - 1800,* edited by J. A. Mazzeo (New York, 1962); Irvin Ehrenpreis, "The Meaning of Gulliver's Last Voyage," *Review of English Literature,* III (1962), 18 - 38; James E. Gill, "Beast Over Man: Theriophilic Paradox in Gulliver's 'Voyage to the Country of the Houyhnhnms,' " *Studies in Philology,* LXVII (1970), 532 - 49; and the previously cited work by Carnochan.

5. When, as here, a reference to *Hudibras* is cited by only canto and line, the passage is taken from Part I of the poem.

6. Butler's Commonplace Book, p. 80a, quoted by Bentley, "Hudibras Butler," p. 85.

7. The literary use of the conception of animals as machines has been treated by Wallace Shugg in "The Cartesian Beast-Machine in English Literature (1663 - 1750)," *Journal of the History of Ideas,* XXIX (1968), 279 - 92. Butler receives little more than passing mention in this study. See also Leonora Cohen Rosenfield, *From Beast-Machine to Man-Machine: Animal Soul in French Letters from Descartes to La Mettrie* (New York, 1941).

8. Boas, pp. 1 - 2.

9. Wilders, Commentary, p. 323.

10. Though I shall draw upon evidence from Part II to establish Butler's interest in the ambiguous relations between men and beasts, I do not here include the latter two parts of *Hudibras* in the present interpretation of the satire. For an interpretation that makes more of the differences between the three parts of *Hudibras,* see W. O. S. Sutherland, Jr., pp. 54 - 71.

11. See Butler's note to I, i, 529 - 30.

12. See Butler's note to I, iii, 134.

13. The words are Daniel Toutville's, quoted by C. A. Patrides, *Milton and the Christian Tradition* (Oxford, 1966), p. 67.

14. Cf. Marvell's definition of a skimmington: "A Punishment invented first to awe/Masculine Wives, transgressing Natural l aw ' "Last Instructions to a Painter," quoted by Wilders, Commentary, p. 386.

15. John Milton, *Works,* edited by Frank A. Patterson (New York, 1931 - 40), III, 475.

16. Quoted by John Halkell in *Milton and the Idea of Matrimony* (New Haven, 1970), p. 52.

17. *Satires and Miscellaneous Poetry and Prose,* p. 220.

18. *Ibid.,* p. 211.

Chapter Five

1. A. H. de Quehen has identified "A Covetous Man" as an early version of "A Miser." The two fugitive *characters* may be found on pp. 472 - 74 and 479 - 80 in Waller's *Characters and Passages from Note-Books.*
2. *Genuine Remains,* II, iv.
3. Benjamin Boyce, *The Polemic Character, 1640 - 1661* (Lincoln, 1955), p. 8. See also David Nichol Smith, *Characters from the Histories & Memoirs of the Seventeenth Century* (Oxford, 1928), pp. xxix - xxx.
4. Smith, *Ibid.*
5. Daves, ed., *Characters,* p. 17. I am indebted to Daves for the analogues in Earle and Cleveland mentioned in this paragraph.
6. W. J. Paylor, *The Overburian Characters* (Oxford, 1936), p. vii.
7. Jack, p. 31.
8. Bentley, "Hudibras Butler," p. 86.

Chapter Six

1. Quoted by Bond, p. 34.
2. *The Poems of John Cleveland,* edited by Brian Morris and Eleanor Withington (Oxford, 1967), p. 180.
3. Bond, p. 263.
4. *Ibid.,* p. 265.
5. *Ibid.,* p. 319.
6. Included in *Poems on Affairs of State,* edited by Galbraith M. Crump (New Haven, 1968), V, 330 - 33.
7. Richards, p. 41.
8. I rely upon Richards for the titles cited in this paragraph.
9. Elizabeth Cook, *Literary Influences in Colonial Newspapers* (New York, 1912), p. 134.
10. Bruce Ingham Granger, "Hudibras in the American Revolution," *American Literature,* XXVII (1956), 499 - 508.
11. Quoted in *Ibid.,* p. 507.
12. *The Satiric Poems of John Trumbull,* edited by Edwin T. Bowden (Austin, 1962), p. 103.
13. Richards, p. 111
14. Earl Miner, *The Restoration Mode from Milton to Dryden* (Princeton, 1974), pp. 159, 196.
15. *Ibid.,* p. 183.

Selected Bibliography

1. Collections

The Poetical Works of Samuel Butler. Memoir of Butler by Rev. John Mit-
ford. 2 vols. Boston: Little, Brown, and Co., 1853. Contains *Hudibras*
and the poems in the *Genuine Remains.* Reissued in one volume by
Houghton, Mifflin and Co., n.d.
The Poetical Works of Samuel Butler. Introduction and notes by Rev.
George Gilfillan. 2 vols. New York: D. Appleton and Co., 1854. Con-
tains *Hudibras,* the poems in the *Genuine Remains,* and "Various
Readings and Additions to *Hudibras.*"
Hudibras Parts I and II and Selected Other Writings. Edited by John
Wilders and Hugh de Quehen. Oxford: Clarendon Press, 1973.
Includes "The Elephant in the Moon," "Satire upon the Royal
Society," several *characters,* and passages from Butler's notebooks.
Fully annotated with bibliography. The only available paperback of
Butler.

2. Editions of *Hudibras*

Hudibras. Troy, N.Y.: Wright, Goodenow, and Stockwell, 1806. First
American edition.
Hudibras, by Samuel Butler. Life, preface, and annotations by Zachary
Grey. 3 vols. London: Charles and Henry Baldwyn, 1819. Contains
selections from translations of *Hudibras,* plates, woodcuts, and
valuable index.
Hudibras by Samuel Butler. Memoir and notes by Treadway Russell Nash.
New York: 1847.
Hudibras, by Samuel Butler. Edited with an introduction by Henry G.
Bohn. London: Bell and Sons, 1882. Contains notes by Grey and
Nash, woodcuts by Thurston, and an index. Reissued 1907.

Hudibras. Edited by A. R. Waller. Cambridge: Cambridge University Press, 1905. Wanting any sort of editorial commentary, this edition is wholly supplanted by the following one.
Hudibras. Edited with an introduction and commentary by John Wilders. Oxford: Clarendon Press, 1967. Contains Butler's letter to George Oxenden and an index. The standard text of the poem.

3. Other Works

Characters and Passages from Note-Books. Edited by A. R. Waller. Cambridge: Cambridge University Press, 1908. Most complete text available of selected prose from Butler's notebook.
Samuel Butler: Satires and Miscellaneous Poetry and Prose. Edited by René Lamar. Cambridge: Cambridge University Press, 1928. Most complete text of Butler's miscellaneous verse.
Samuel Butler: Three Poems. Edited with an introduction by Alexander C. Spence. Augustan Reprint Society Publication no. 88. Los Angeles: Clark Memorial Library, 1961. Includes facsimilies of "To the Memory of . . . Du-Vall," "Satyr on Our Ridiculous Imitation of the French," and "The Elephant in the Moon."
Samuel Butler 1612 - 1680: Characters. Edited by Charles W. Daves. Cleveland: Press of Case Western Reserve Universities, 1970. Standard edition of Butler's *characters.* Contains useful commentary.

SECONDARY SOURCES

ANDERSON, P. B. "Anonymous Critic of Milton: Richard Leigh? or Butler?" *Studies in Philology,* XLIV (1947), 504 - 18. Convincing argument for Butler's authorship of *The Character of the Rump, The Censure of the Rota Upon Mr. Milton's Book . . . . ,* and *The Transproser Rehears'd.*
AUBREY, JOHN. *Brief Lives.* Edited by Andrew Clark. 2 vols. Oxford: Clarendon Press, 1898. Biographical notes by Butler's acquaintance.
BALDWIN, EDWARD CHAUNCEY. "A Suggestion for a New Edition of Butler's *Hudibras.*" *Publications of the Modern Language Association,* XXVI (1911), 528 - 48. The starting point of modern bibliographical study of *Hudibras.*
BAUER, JOSEPHINE. "Some Verse Fragments and Prose *Characters* by Samuel Butler Not Included in the Complete Works." *Modern Philology,* XLV (1948), 160 - 68. Pieces together the fragments of Butler's unfinished poem on medicine.
BENTLEY, NORMA E. "A Grant to 'Hudibras' Butler." *Modern Language Notes,* LIX (1944), 281. On Charles II's "free guift" to Butler in 1680.
———. "Another Butler Manuscript." *Modern Philology,* XLIV (1948),

132 - 35. Describes Butler's *Manuscript Commonplace Book;* reprints the then uncollected character of "A Schoolmaster."

————. "Hudibras Butler." Doctoral dissertation, Syracuse University, 1944. Primarily a study of Butler's thought, but also contains biographical and critical material. Includes copious quotation from Manuscript Commonplace book.

————. " 'Hudibras' Butler Abroad." *Modern Language Notes,* XL (1945), 254 - 59. Presents evidence of Butler's trip to France in 1670.

BLUNDEN, EDMUND. "Some Remarks on *Hudibras.*" *London Mercury,* XVIII (1928), 172 - 77. Negligible piece of subjective appreciation.

BOND, RICHMOND P. *English Burlesque Poetry: 1700 - 1750.* Cambridge, Mass.: Harvard University Press, 1932. Survey of the "Hudibrastic" form in English burlesque poetry. Contains a "Register of Burlesque Poems" from 1700 - 1750.

BOYCE, BENJAMIN. *The Polemic Character: 1640 - 1661.* Lincoln: University of Nebraska Press, 1955. "Postscript: From Polemic Character to Verse Satire: *Hudibras,* Part I" traces the relationship between Butler's poem and the satiric rhetoric of the later prose *character.*

BRUUN, SV. "Who's Who in Samuel Butler's *The Elephant in the Moon.*" *English Studies,* L (1969), 381 - 89. Opposes Marjorie Nicolson's identification of the personages in Butler's satire on the Royal Society.

C. V. H. *The Vigornian* (November 1921). On Butler's education at the King's School in Worcester.

CHEW, BEVERLY. "Some Notes on the Three Parts of *Hudibras.*" *The Bibliographer,* I (1902), 123 - 38. Superficial consideration of bibliographical problems in the poem.

CRAIG, HARDIN. "*Hudibras,* Part I, and the Politics of 1647." In *The Manly Anniversary Studies in Language and Literature,* pp. 145 - 55. Chicago: University of Chicago Press, 1923. Attempts to date the composition of Part I of the poem using internal evidence.

CUNNINGHAM, PETER. "The Author of Hudibras at Ludlow Castle." *Notes and Queries,* 1st ser., V (1852), 5 - 6. Reprints evidence of Butler's employment as steward for Richard Vaughn.

CURTISS, JOSEPH T. "Butler's *Sidrophel.*" *Publications of the Modern Language Association,* XLIV (1929), 1066 - 78. Development of Sidrophel as a satirical portrait. Butler's early ridicule of the astrologer William Lilly was made to accommodate the Royal Society member, Sir Paul Neile.

DAVIES, PAUL C. "*Hudibras* and the "proper Sphere of Wit." *Trivium,* V (1970), 104 - 15. Uses Butler's definition of "wit" as a point of departure for critical consideration of *Hudibras.*

DE QUEHEN, A. H. "Editing Butler's Manuscripts." In *Editing Seventeenth-Century Prose.* Edited by D. I. B. Smith, pp. 71 - 93. Toronto: Hakkert, 1972. Brilliant exercise in the textual criticism of Butler's notebook material.

DUFFETT, G. W. "The Name 'Hudibras.'" *Notes and Queries*, IX (1935), 96. Finds the source of Hudibras' name in Jonson's *The New Inn*.

ERSKINE-HILL, H. H. "Edmund Waller and Samuel Butler: Two Poetic Debts to Hall's Occasional Meditations." *Notes and Queries*, XII (1965), 133 - 34. Butler's borrowing in Part I *Hudibras* (i) from Hall's "Occasionall Meditations" (110).

GIBSON, DAN, JR. "Samuel Butler." In *Seventeenth Century Studies by Members of the Graduate School, University of Cincinatti*, edited by Robert Shafer. Princeton: Princeton University Press for the University of Cincinatti, 1933. Reviews Butler's thinking on religion, science, and poetry.

GRANGER, BRUCE INGHAM. "Hudibras in the American Revolution." *American Literature*, XXVII (1956), 499 - 508. Surveys the influence of *Hudibras* in eighteenth century American verse.

HINDLE, C. J. "A Broadside by Samuel Butler." *Times Literary Supplement*, March 21, 1936, p. 244. Argues the case of Butler's authorship of *Lord Roos His Answer*.

HORNE, WILLIAM C. "Butler's Use of the *Rump* in *Hudibras*." *Library Chronicle*, XXXVII (1971), 126 - 35. "*Hudibras* seems the ultimate development of a stock figure, a type of Round-head *miles gloriosus*" who originated in *Rump*, a Royalist anthology of satirical verse.

JACK, IAN. "Low Satire: *Hudibras*." In *Augustan Satire: Intention and Idiom in English Poetry: 1600 - 1750*. Oxford: Clarendon Press, 1952. Excellent study of the general characteristics of Butler's satire. "*Hudibras* is the opposite of the mock-heroic."

JOHNSON, SAMUEL. "Butler." In *Lives of the English Poets*. 2 vols. London, 1954. Biographical and critical commentary.

KENNAN, HUGH T. "Another 'Hudibras' Allusion in Byron's 'Don Juan.'" *Notes and Queries*, XIV (1967), 301 - 02. On a borrowing in *Don Juan* (VIII) from the argument to Part I *Hudibras* (i).

KULISHECK, C. L. "Hudibrastic Echoes in Swift." *Notes and Queries*, CXCVI (1951), 339. Assumes Swift's familiarity with passages now available only in Butler's notebooks.

LAMAR, RENÉ. "Du Nouveau sur l'auteur d'*Hudibras*': Samuel Butler en Worcestershire." *La Revue Anglo-Americaine*, I (1924), 213 - 27. Valuable source of information on Butler's ancestry and early life.

———. "Samuel Butler à l'École du Roi." *Etudes anglaises*, V (1952), 17 - 24. Cautious speculation in the obscure area of Butler's early life.

———. "Samuel Butler et la Justice de son Temps." *Etudes anglaises*, VII (1954), 271 - 79. Considers Butler's attitude toward law and the legal profession.

LEYBURN, ELLEN DOUGLASS. "*Hudibras* Considered as Satiric Allegory." *Huntington Library Quarterly*, XVI (1953). Reprinted in *Satiric Allegory: Mirror of Man*. New Haven: Yale University Press, 1956. Butler's characters stand for habits of mind, not historical personages.

MILLER, WARD S. "The Allegory in Part I of *Hudibras.*" *Huntington Library Quarterly*, XXI (1958), 323 - 43. Interesting, but perhaps over-ingenious interpretation of *Hudibras* as both anti-Puritan and anti-Royalist satire. Presents some surprising contemporary parallels of images in *Hudibras*.

MINER, EARL. *The Restoration Mode from Milton to Dryden.* Princeton: Princeton University Press, 1974. Published too late for consideration in the present volume, Miner's chapter on Butler anticipates a number of its ideas.

NEVO, RUTH. *The Dial of Virtue: A Study of Poems on Affairs of State in the Seventeenth Century.* Princeton: Princeton University Press, 1963. Determines a key position for *Hudibras* in the evolution of seventeenth century political satire.

NICOLSON, MARJORIE HOPE. *Pepys' Diary and the New Science.* Charlottesville: University of Virginia Press, 1965. Sheds considerable light on the personages and events behind Butler's satires on science and the Royal Society.

PAULSON, RONALD. *Hogarth: His Life, Art, and Times.* London: Yale University Press, 1971. Paulson's chapter on Hogarth's illustrations of *Hudibras* provides an interesting approach to the poem.

QUINTANA, RICARDO. "Samuel Butler: A Restoration Figure in a Modern Light." *English Literary History*, XVIII (1951), 7 - 31. Surveys Butler's place, as both satirist and moralist, in the history of Augustine literature. The first major modern study of the satirist; still an important one.

―――. "The Butler-Oxenden Correspondance." *Modern Language Notes*, XLVIII (1933), 1 - 11. Primary evidence on the composition of *Hudibras*. The most important discovery in modern Butler scholarship.

―――. "John Hall of Durham and Samuel Butler: A Note." *Modern Language Notes*, XLIV (1929), 176 - 79. Suggested borrowings by Butler from Hall's *A Satire*, published 1646.

RICHARDS, EDWARD AMES. *Hudibras in the Burlesque Tradition.* Columbia University Studies in English and Comparative Literature, no. 127. New York: Columbia University Press, 1937. Surveys the imitations of *Hudibras* in England, Scotland, and America. Chapter I, on Butler's personality, is perhaps the most perceptive treatment the poet has received. Contains a valuable bibliography of "hudibrastic verse" to 1830.

SEIDEL, MICHAEL, A. "Patterns of Anarchy and Oppression in Samuel Butler's *Hudibras.*" *Eighteenth-Century Studies*, V (1971), 294 - 314. In place of the conventional thesis-antithesis structure of most satire, *Hudibras* presents a pattern of social extremes, both of which are satirized.

SUTHERLAND, W. O. S., JR. *The Art of the Satirist: Essays on the Satire of*

Augustan England. Austin: University of Texas, 1965. Interesting chapter on *Hudibras* as a general satire on human nature.

THORSON, JAMES L. "The Publication of *Hudibras*," *Papers of the Bibliographical Society of America*, LX (1966), 418 - 38. Bibliographical study of the three parts of *Hudibras*.

———. "Samuel Butler (1612 - 1680): A Bibliography." *Bulletin of Bibliography*, XXX (1973) 34 - 39. "Attempt at a complete bibliography" of biographical, bibliographical, and critical information on Butler. Also includes a list of "Editions of note."

VELDKAMP, JAN. *Samuel Butler, The Author of Hudibras.* Hilversum: Drukkerij "DeAtlas," 1923. Generally dated, but still useful for its treatment of the religious and historical background of the poem and of Butler's relationship to Cervantes and Rabelais.

WASSERMAN, GEORGE R. "A Strange Chimaera of Beasts and Men." *Studies in English Literature*, XIII (1973), pp. 405 - 21. Study of the argument and imagery of Part I of *Hudibras*. A shorter version of the fourth chapter of the present study.

———. "Samuel Butler and the Problem of Unnatural Man." *Modern Language Quarterly*, XXXI (1970), 179 - 94. Considers Butler's interest in human reason as the means of unnatural behavior in men. This thesis is treated in greater detail in the second chapter of the present study.

WEBSTER, C. M. "*Hudibras* and Swift." *Modern Language Notes*, XLVII (1932), 245 - 46. On a borrowing from Part I *Hudibras* (ii, 367) in Swift's *Baucis and Philemon*.

WILDING, MICHAEL. "Samuel Butler at Barbourne." *Notes and Queries*, XIII (1966), 15 - 19. Biographical information on Butler's early schooldays.

WILDING, R. M. "The Date of Samuel Butler's Baptism." *Review of English Studies*, XVII (1966), 174 - 77. Newly found information on the Butler family.

WOOD, ANTHONY à. *Athenae Oxonienses.* Edited by Philip Bliss. 5 vols. London: F. G. & J. Rivington, 1813 - 20. Biographical notes by one of Butler's contemporaries.

Index